Hail to the Chiefs

Celebrating Kansas City's World Championship

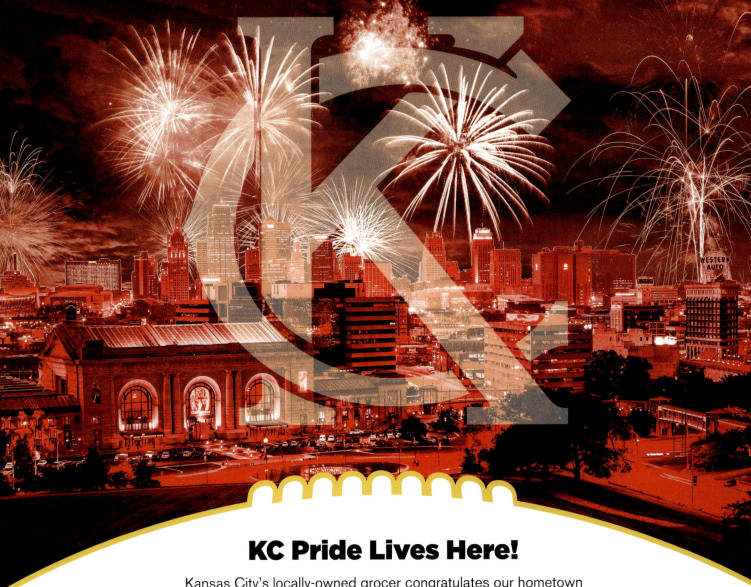

CONGRATULATIONS!

KC Pride Lives Here!

Kansas City's locally-owned grocer congratulates our hometown football team and the best fans in the nation on an incredible season. Thanks for bringing sports glory to our city and giving us all a reason to celebrate!

Proud to be Kansas City owned

INTRO	4
Super Bowl | **SAN FRANCISCO**	6
Regular Season | **JACKSONVILLE**	16
Regular Season | **OAKLAND**	20
Regular Season | **BALTIMORE**	26
KC Feature | **TRAVIS KELCE**	30
Regular Season | **DETROIT**	32
Regular Season | **INDIANAPOLIS**	38
KC Feature | **TYREEK HILL**	42
Regular Season | **HOUSTON**	44
Regular Season | **DENVER**	50
Regular Season | **GREEN BAY**	54
KC Feature | **TYRANN MATHIEU**	58
Regular Season | **MINNESOTA**	62
Regular Season | **TENNESSEE**	66
Regular Season | **L.A. CHARGERS**	70
KC Feature | **HEAD COACH ANDY REID**	76
Regular Season | **OAKLAND**	80
Regular Season | **NEW ENGLAND**	84
Regular Season | **DENVER**	90
KC Feature | **PATRICK MAHOMES**	94
Regular Season | **CHICAGO**	98
Regular Season | **L.A. CHARGERS**	104
AFC Divisional Playoff | **HOUSTON**	110
AFC Championship | **TENNESSEE**	118
SUPER BOWL 1970	126
KANSAS CITY CHIEFS ROSTER	128

ANDREA ZAGATA, *Cover Design* | **NICKY BRILLOWSKI**, *Book Design*

© 2020 KCI Sports Publishing

All rights reserved. Except for use in a review, the reproduction or utilization of this work in any form or by any electronic, mechanical, or other means, now known or hereafter invented, including xerography, photocopying, and recording, and in any information storage and retrieval system, is forbidden without the written permission of the publisher.

Printed in the United States of America

This is an unofficial publication. This book is in no way affiliated with, licensed by or endorsed by the Kansas City Chiefs or the National Football League.

INTRODUCTION

At Last

Kansas City Chiefs - World Champions!

Sounds pretty good doesn't it? Kansas City fans have waited 50 long years to utter those words, and finally, the Chiefs are back on top.

Let the celebration begin!

It is an honor to be able to chronicle such a historic season. This was a championship season that had been 12 months in the making. Following last year's devasting overtime loss to the New England Patriots in the AFC Championship Game, GM Brett Veach an Coach Any Reid headed into the offseason with one goal in mind—building a team that could win Super Bowl LIV.

Mission accomplished.

The Chiefs went all in by making some tough personnel decisions on a number of veterans following the 2018-19 season while restocking their roster with talented, young players like Tyrann Mathieu, Frank Clark, Besahud Breeland, and Alex Okafor that gave new defensive coordinator Steve Spagnuolo the pieces to overhaul and upgrade the defense. The offense remained a powerhouse - unstoppable at times - and when injuries struck the "next man up" was always ready to go. Perhaps no player exemplified that better than backup quarterback Matt Moore, who went 2-1 as the starter following a knee injury to Patrick Mahomes in Denver that had Chiefs Kingdom thinking the season was lost. The perseverance, teamwork and will to win that made up the DNA of this Chiefs team was on full display week after week.

In the following pages we proudly take you on a trip down memory lane of this championship season that came to its jubilant conclusion with the Super Bowl LIV victory in Miami over a very talented San Francisco 49ers team.

Heartfelt congratulations go out to the Hunt family, GM Brett Veach, Coach Andy Reid and his staff, and the entire team on their incredible accomplishments this season. Celebrate this season Kansas City fans, and save this book to revisit the Chiefs' magical moments and this unforgettable team – both stars and role players – who rewarded your faith with an NFL Championship.

Congratulations Chiefs Kingdom! Let's do it again soon. ∎

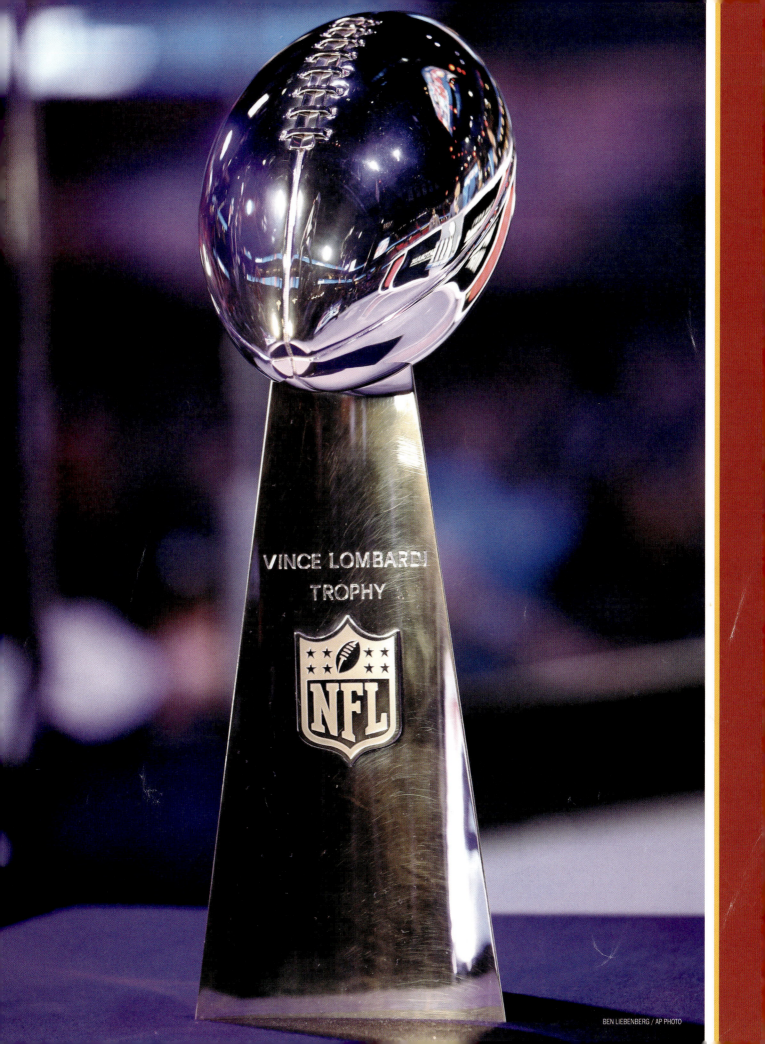

BEN LIEBENBERG / AP PHOTO

KANSAS CITY 31, SAN FRANCISCO 20
FEBRUARY 2, 2020 | MIAMI GARDENS, FLORIDA

World Champions!
Chiefs rally to win first Super Bowl in 50 years

Patrick Mahomes keeps rewriting the NFL history books, and the wait for the Chiefs – and for their head coach – is finally over.

A half century after winning their first, the Kansas City Chiefs have won Super Bowl LIV, defeating the San Francisco 49ers 31-20 at Hard Rock Stadium.

Mahomes, last year's league MVP, is now a Super Bowl MVP. He has joined Ben Roethlisberger and Tom Brady as the only quarterbacks to hoist a Lombardi Trophy before their 25th birthday.

At 24 years and 138 days old on Sunday, Mahomes became the fifth-youngest quarterback to start in the Super Bowl. He's also now the youngest player to win both an NFL MVP award and a Super Bowl title, surpassing Pro Football Hall of Famer Emmitt Smith (24 years, 233 days old on the last day of his MVP 1993 season).

"It's like watching Denzel [Washington] in a movie. It's like watching LeBron James in the playoffs," Chiefs safety Tyrann Mathieu said. "He has that spark. For him to be that young and to find the confidence to do what he did against a special defense, that tells you everything you need to know about that man."

And it's the first title for Andy Reid, 61, who up until Sunday night had been known as the best head coach to have never won a Super Bowl or NFL championship. This was his second Super Bowl appearance in his 21-year head coaching career.

Now, with career win No. 222, Reid is a champion. He broke the record for the most wins (including the playoffs) by a head coach before winning a Super Bowl or NFL championship, surpassing 2020 Pro Football Hall of Famer Bill Cowher's 152 wins.

"Nobody deserves this trophy more than Andy Reid," Chiefs chairman Clark Hunt said.

Mahomes magic

It wasn't easy for the Chiefs. For the third straight game, Kansas City trailed by double digits, down 20-10 in the fourth quarter. That was, in part, because Mahomes was pressured by the 49ers defensive front and was sacked four times.

With 5:23 left in the third quarter, Mahomes made his first big mistake, throwing his first career postseason interception, setting up a 49ers touchdown to make it 20-10. He was picked off again on Kansas City's next

Chiefs quarterback Patrick Mahomes raises the Lombardi Trophy as he celebrates the Super Bowl LIV win. ANTHONY BEHAR / AP PHOTO

Chiefs quarterback Patrick Mahomes (15) scores on a 1-yard run as 49ers' linebacker Kwon Alexander (56) attempts to defend. WILFREDO LEE / AP PHOTO

ABOVE: Chiefs running back Damien Williams (26) reaches the nose of the ball across the goal line giving Kansas City a 24-20 lead late in the fourth quarter. MARK HUMPHREY / AP PHOTO

OPPOSITE: Chiefs defensive back Bashaud Breeland (21) makes a huge interception on a pass by 49ers quarterback Jimmy Garoppolo. WILFREDO LEE / AP PHOTO

possession, with a Mahomes throw going behind wide receiver Tyreek Hill and snared by Tarvarius Moore.

Mahomes' 11 passing touchdowns without an interception was the most to start a playoff career in the Super Bowl era.

"They're one of the best defenses that I've been up against in my career so far," Mahomes said of the 49ers.

But as it got late, Mahomes got to work, with three straight touchdown drives in just over five minutes.

With 6:13 left, Mahomes found Travis Kelce in the endzone to cut it to 3. And with 2:44 remaining, Mahomes hit Damien Williams with a 5-yard pass for the go-ahead score. It was a play that would be reviewed, as it appeared Williams may have stepped out of bounds before the ball crossed the plane, but the call stood.

On that drive, Mahomes went 5-for-5 for 60 yards. For the night, Mahomes completed 26 of his 42 passes for 286 yards.

A breakaway touchdown run of 38 yards by Williams put the game away with 1:12 left.

"We never give up," Mahomes said. "I think those guys, the leaders that we have on this team, they have that mindset that we never give up and we're going to fight until the end.

"Thank you, Kansas City. We did it, baby!"

Mahomes became just the third black starting quarterback to win Super Bowl MVP, joining Doug Williams and Russell Wilson.

"The best thing about it is you're showing kids that no matter where you grow up, what race you are, that you can achieve your dream," Mahomes said. "For me, being a black quarterback – having a black dad and a white mom – it just shows that it doesn't matter where you come from. It doesn't matter if you're a baseball player or basketball player, follow your dreams.

"Whatever your dreams are, put the work ethic in and you can be there at the end of the day." ∎

Frank Clark and Patrick Mahomes celebrate the Super Bowl victory.
KEVIN C. COX / GETTY IMAGES

The World Champion Kansas City Chiefs.
MORRY GASH / AP PHOTO

KANSAS CITY 40, JACKSONVILLE 26

SEPTEMBER 8, 2019 | JACKSONVILLE, FLORIDA

Overpowering Opener
Mahomes, Chiefs too much for Jags

Patrick Mahomes was every bit as good as he was during his MVP campaign. Sammy Watkins was better than ever.

Mahomes and Watkins – along with new teammate LeSean McCoy – helped the Kansas City Chiefs open the season much like they finished last year: as legitimate Super Bowl contenders.

Despite losing star receiver Tyreek Hill early, Mahomes threw for 378 yards and three touchdowns while leading the Chiefs to a testy and tactful 40-26 victory over the injury-riddled Jacksonville Jaguars on Sunday.

"They've done that to a lot of football teams," Jaguars coach Doug Marrone said.

Jacksonville had major issues on both sides of the ball, none more concerning than the health of quarterback Nick Foles. Foles broke his left clavicle in the first quarter and will have surgery Monday. Chris Jones hit Foles as he released a 35-yard TD pass to DJ Chark. Jones landed on top of Foles, but did not draw a flag.

Foles is expected to be put on injured reserve and won't be eligible to play again until Week 11.

"It's not the way you want to start your time here," said Foles, who signed a four-year, $88 million contract in March.

The injury leaves rookie Gardner Minshew in line to start a significant chunk of Jacksonville's season. Minshew was one of the team's few bright spots. He completed 22 of 25 passes for 275 yards, with two touchdowns and an interception.

Mahomes completed passes to nine receivers with Watkins having most of the highlights.

Watkins had nine receptions for a career-high 198 yards and three TDs. He slipped through the middle of Jacksonville's defense for a 68-yard score on the third play of the season and added a 49-yard TD reception late in the opening quarter. He made defenders Ronnie Harrison, Jalen Ramsey and Miles Jack look silly while strolling into the end zone twice. He beat Ramsey again for a short TD in the fourth quarter.

Mahomes took a beating even though he wasn't sacked and even had to leave the game to get his left ankle taped in the second quarter.

Chiefs safety Armani Watts, top, leaps high over the Jaguars Andrew Wingard (42) to grab an onside kick. STEPHEN B. MORTON / AP PHOTO

It barely slowed him and the Chiefs down; they scored on their first seven possessions.

McCoy carried 10 times for 81 yards despite barely knowing the offense.

"We have a mindset throughout the season of taking care of certain goals and this was one of them," Chiefs All-Pro tight end Travis Kelce said. "Just come out blazing, on fire, like we were last year. ... I think we're on the right track and we're going to keep working to get where we want to be."

Jaguars linebacker Jack was ejected in the second quarter after taking a swing at Chiefs receiver Demarcus Robinson. Jack had to be restrained by team officials and essentially pulled off the field.

Jack and Watkins got into a shoving match after a fumble, and then Robinson came in and shoved Jack in the back. Ramsey and others joined in, prompting officials to throw five flags and a hat onto the ground. Jack eventually got the boot after a lengthy discussion.

Frank Clark, who recorded 35 sacks the last four years with Seattle, made his Chiefs debut and had an interception off a tipped pass. Clark signed a five-year, $104 million deal to join Kansas City in free agency.

"I've got more picks than Jalen Ramsey right now so that's a highlight," Clark joked. ∎

Chiefs running back Damien Williams (26) celebrates in the end zone after rushing for a third-quarter touchdown.
PHELAN M. EBENHACK / AP PHOTO

KANSAS CITY 28, OAKLAND 10
SEPTEMBER 15, 2019 | OAKLAND, CALIFORNIA

Chiefs Rout Raiders
Mahomes stays hot with 4 TDs

Patrick Mahomes bounced back from the first scoreless opening quarter of his career in the regular season by throwing four touchdown passes in a near perfect second period that led the Kansas City Chiefs to a 28-10 victory over the Oakland Raiders on Sunday.

The Raiders (1-1) held Mahomes in check for the opening 15 minutes before he carved up an overmatched defense with big play after big play in the second quarter for the Chiefs (2-0).

Mahomes didn't take long to strike, finding Demarcus Robinson open on a blown coverage for a 44-yard touchdown pass on the first play in the second quarter. He didn't slow down from there.

After the Raiders opted to punt on a fourth-and-1 near midfield, Mahomes and the Chiefs marched 95 yards and scored when Mahomes found rookie Mecole Hardman on a 42-yard deep strike for his first career catch to give Kansas City a 14-10 lead.

The Chiefs didn't stop there with Mahomes connecting on two more long TD passes in the final two minutes of the half, a 27-yarder to Travis Kelce and a 39-yarder to Robinson as the absence of injured star Tyreek Hill did little to slow Kansas City. Mahomes' 278 yards passing in the second quarter were the most for a player in any quarter since Drew Brees had 294 in the fourth period against Atlanta on Nov. 9, 2008.

"We were just hitting on the plays," Mahomes said. "We hit a lot of them in the second quarter, and we missed them in other parts of the game."

"We had breakdowns in coverage, and a couple of those were just incredible throws and catches," Raiders coach Jon Gruden said. "You have to tip your hat to them. We didn't get enough pressure. You have to blame the coaches for that. We got (Mahomes) a couple times, but not consistently enough. We let him move around back there and cock his arm, and when he gets an opportunity to do that he can drop them in no matter where they are. We ran into a buzz saw for about seven minutes."

"Those first two (touchdowns), we just gave them by not (communicating)," Raiders safety Lamarcus Joyner said. "Those guys are going to scheme you up and make plays — they're arguably the best offense in the NFL — but more games are lost than won, and you can't just give a team like that big plays."

Mahomes finished 30 for 44 for 443 yards

Raiders tight end Darren Waller is driven out of bounds by Chiefs cornerback Kendall Fuller (29) during the second half. BEN MARGOT / AP PHOTO

on the day. Robinson had six catches for 172 yards and two scores and Kelce had seven catches for 107 yards and a TD to give the Chiefs their ninth win in the past 10 meetings in this long-time rivalry.

"Today my number was called," Robinson said. "I got a chance to make some plays, and I did."

Robinson figured to become more involved in the absence of Hill, who was absent from the lineup with a shoulder injury.

With Mahomes at the controls, anyone can post big numbers.

"Any week can be a big week for any one of us," Robinson said. "We don't go out thinking it's Mecole's week or Sammy's week or my week or Kelce's week. It could be anyone."

The Raiders had broken out to a 10-0 lead with a field goal on the opening drive and a 4-yard TD pass to Tyrell Williams later in the first quarter. But Carr also threw an interception in the end zone on a pass to Williams in the third quarter and the Raiders didn't score over the final three periods.

"That's a good defense," Carr said. "They were up so big last week they were playing a different style of game. They bring a lot of exotic pressures and it's hit or miss sometimes."

The victory marked the Chiefs' ninth over Oakland in the last 10 meetings between the two teams, and in Kansas City's last visit to The Black Hole before the Raiders move to Las Vegas in 2020, the Chiefs secured the all-time series at the Oakland-Alameda County Coliseum with a record of 22-20-1. ∎

Chiefs tight end Travis Kelce (87) beats Oakland defenders Karl Joseph (42) and Erik Harris (25) for a 27-yard touchdown reception during the second quarter. RIC TAPIA / AP PHOTO

Chiefs wide receiver Demarcus Robinson (11) is greeted by teammate Damien Williams (26) after scoring on a 39-yard touchdown reception. BEN MARGOT / AP PHOTO

KANSAS CITY 33, BALTIMORE 28

SEPTEMBER 22, 2019 | KANSAS CITY, MISSOURI

Next Man Up

Shorthanded Chiefs hold off Ravens

The Kansas City Chiefs rolled into Arrowhead Stadium to play the red-hot Baltimore Ravens without their best wide receiver, their lead running back and their stalwart left tackle.

They still had Patrick Mahomes, though.

The reigning league MVP threw for 374 yards and three touchdowns in another record-setting performance, and Kansas City's defense corralled Ravens quarterback Lamar Jackson most of the rain-soaked afternoon, allowing the Chiefs to squeak out a 33-28 victory Sunday.

"Everyone gets reps with the starters, and guys just build that confidence that they can play," said Mahomes, whose 13 games of at least 300 yards passing broke Kurt Warner's mark for the most in the first 20 games of a career. "Whenever someone gets an opportunity they make plays."

Such as wide receivers Demarcus Robinson and Mecole Hardman, who had TD catches while Tyreek Hill recovers from a broken collarbone. Or LeSean McCoy and Darrell Williams, who combined for 116 yards rushing and a score in place of injured running back Damien Williams. Or Cam Erving, who filled in for left tackle Eric Fisher and helped to limit the Ravens to a single sack.

"I trust that guys are going to step up and play," said Chiefs coach Andy Reid, whose 210th win broke a tie with Chuck Knoll for sixth-most in NFL history. "Each one of them collectively had a pretty good day. They took advantage of their opportunity."

Missed opportunities ultimately doomed the Ravens. They were stuffed once on fourth down, and three times they failed to convert on a 2-point conversion, leaving them chasing points all game.

The last came after Jackson scrambled for a touchdown with 2:01 to go. The conversion would have gotten the Ravens (2-1) within a field goal, but Jackson was shoved out of bounds short of the pylon.

Baltimore tried to get the ball back with a rare dropkick, but the Chiefs (3-0) calmly called for a fair catch. Then they converted on third down moments later to run out the clock.

"I don't remember the situation or which was what, but every one of those was clear analytical decisions to go for two," Ravens coach John Harbaugh said. "We had a mindset that we were going to come in and try to score as many points as we could. So, that's what we tried to do."

Chiefs quarterback Patrick Mahomes (15) celebrates after completing a pass for a first down during the second half. ED ZURGA / AP PHOTO

Mark Ingram was the Ravens' biggest bright spot, running for 103 yards and a trio of touchdowns while catching four passes for 32 yards. Jackson finished with 267 yards passing and 46 rushing, most of that when he was trying to rally the Ravens from a big halftime hole.

The Ravens actually scored first on Ingram's touchdown plunge, then they took points off the board when a penalty gave them a shorter try at the conversion. Jackson was stuffed at the goal line in what would become a recurring theme for Baltimore all afternoon.

The Chiefs then proceeded to score four times in the second quarter for the second consecutive week, this time getting three touchdowns and Harrison Butker's 42-yard field goal to take a 23-6 lead.

McCoy, hobbled by a sore ankle all week, gave Kansas City the lead with a TD run early in the second quarter. Then, after the Ravens' turnover on downs, Mahomes lofted a pass to the corner of the end zone that Robinson caught with an incredible one-handed stab.

That highlight was joined by another on the Chiefs' next possession, when the Ravens blew the coverage and Hardman was open downfield. The rookie hauled in the heave from Mahomes, then used his 4.3-second 40-yard-dash speed to sprint 83 yards to the end zone.

"I just did enough to get in the end zone," Hardman said. ∎

Chiefs wide receiver Demarcus Robinson (11) makes a beautiful one-handed 18-yard touchdown catch in front of Ravens cornerback Brandon Carr (24). CHARLIE RIEDEL / AP PHOTO

The Playmaker
Kelce key cog in Chiefs offense

When one thinks of the Kansas City Chiefs offense, the explosive, vertical plays, which result from the big arm of Patrick Mahomes and the speed of Tyreek Hill and Sammy Watkins, come to mind.

But while all three have missed time with injury at some point, tight end Travis Kelce has been the offense's most consistent player.

"He just makes the play," Mahomes said, "and does whatever he can to move the chains."

Often working the middle of the field, Kelce leads the team in receptions (97), targets (152) and yards (1,229) heading into Super Bowl LIV. That receiving yardage mark ranks first among all NFL tight ends and makes him the first tight end in NFL history with four straight 1,000-yard seasons. Even former Chiefs tight end and 2019 Hall of Fame inductee Tony Gonzalez didn't accomplish that. Kelce had shared the record of three consecutive 1,000-yard receiving seasons with Carolina Panthers tight end Greg Olsen, who did it from 2014 to 2016.

While the 34-year-old Olsen is nearing the end of his career, Kelce is still in his prime. The 30-year-old Chiefs tight end is in the midst of a five-year, $46.8 million contract. It goes through the 2021 season, meaning he is slated to become an unrestricted free agent in 2022.

This season he earns a base salary of $7.5 million and carries a cap hit of $10.7 million, which is about 5.65% of the Chiefs' salary cap.

Kansas City is getting its money's worth. They use him all over the field. Kelce even splits wide as a receiver or goes in the slot. In the 23-16 victory against the New England Patriots, he ran for a touchdown while aligned as Wildcat quarterback.

In the play designed by Chiefs offensive line coach Andy Heck, Mahomes lined up behind Kelce. Wide receiver Tyreek Hill was flanked to the tight end's left, and newly-signed running back Spencer Ware was flanked to his right. Kelce had the option to hand it off or run a dive.

"On Travis' end that read was phenomenal," head coach Andy Reid said. "For him to maneuver around everything and get himself in, it was a great job."

After playing quarterback as a freshman at the University of Cincinnati and also during three years in high school, his touchdown against the Patriots represented a return to his former position.

"It was funny because we watched the highlights of him in Cincinnati when he was running the same type of plays," Mahomes said. "I like to take the assist, though, because I kind of held the inside linebacker with my fake."

Though Kelce is known for his elaborate end zone celebrations, Mahomes said he is actually humble and did not brag about his first rushing touchdown.

"No, he doesn't," Mahomes said. "He just loves the game and being a part of the team, and you can see it with how he runs his routes. He's always running hard, trying to get everyone else open. And when he gets his number called, he makes plays." ■

KANSAS CITY 34, DETROIT 30
SEPTEMBER 29, 2019 | DETROIT, MICHIGAN

Road Rally
Darrel Williams TD run keeps Chiefs undefeated

Patrick Mahomes made more plays than usual with his legs because the Detroit Lions set up their defense to limit what the superstar quarterback could do with his arm.

Mahomes converted a fourth down with a run to extend a game-winning drive that ended with Darrel Williams' 1-yard touchdown run with 23 seconds left for his second score in the fourth quarter, lifting the Kansas City Chiefs to a 34-30 win over the Detroit Lions on Sunday.

"With what they were doing, there were lanes to run," Mahomes said. "I saw a lane and I took it."

The reigning MVP had thrown at least two touchdown passes in 14 straight games, one short of the NFL record set by Peyton Manning. And, he was the first player in league history to have at least 350 yards passing and three touchdowns without an interception in three straight games before getting slowed down in Detroit.

"They found a way to take away some of the stuff that we like to do," said Mahomes, who was 24 of 42 for 315 yards. "They hadn't lost a game for a reason."

Kansas City (4-0) stayed undefeated after starting its game-winning drive on the 21 with 2:25 left. Facing fourth-and-8 from the Chiefs 34, Mahomes dropped back briefly before busting through a hole up the middle for 15 yards to help him finish with a career-high 56 yards rushing.

"When they start doubling people, there are going to be some lanes and he knew that," coach Andy Reid said.

The Lions (2-1-1) were determined to take away big plays in Kansas City's passing game, doubling tight end Travis Kelce and receiver Sammy Watkins with some success. The scheme, though, cleared space for Mahomes to run and coach Matt Patricia doesn't regret it.

"If he goes back there and throws it vertical with some of the speed that he has, then I'm not going to be happy," he said.

The plan almost worked.

Kansas City went ahead for the first time early in the third quarter when Bashaud Breeland recovered Kerryon Johnson's fumble and returned it 100 yards, taking advantage of everyone on the field appearing to stop momentarily and the officials not blowing a whistle. The pivotal play stood after review.

"We preach that every day," Breeland said. "You pick up the ball at the end, whether it's

---

Chiefs running back Darrel Williams (31), left, celebrates with offensive tackle Cameron Erving, center, and offensive guard Andrew Wylie (77) after scoring the winning touchdown with :23 seconds left. DUANE BURLESON / AP PHOTO

Chiefs wide receiver Mecole Hardman (17) is brought down by Detroit defenders after making a 7-yard reception. DUANE BURLESON / AP PHOTO

alive or dead. You never know."

The Lions scored the first 10 points and after Kansas City pulled into two ties, they went back ahead late in the second, third and fourth quarters.

Detroit quarterback Matt Stafford threw a 6-yard touchdown pass to Kenny Golladay with 2:26 left to give Detroit a 30-27 lead. The call on the field stood after a review, which showed Golladay got both feet in the end zone. Golladay had a touchdown overturned by review early in the third because it was ruled he did not maintain control of the ball throughout the process of the catch.

Stafford was 21 of 34 for 291 yards with three touchdowns, including two to Golladay and one to T.J. Hockenson. Stafford's second touchdown pass of the game – and first to Golladay – put Detroit up 23-20 and followed a fifth fumble in the third quarter.

"There were a bunch of great plays made in this game, a couple bad plays by each team made in this game," Stafford said. "That's the way it goes in the NFL. It came down to the last 15 seconds. They were undefeated coming into this game. So were we. Somebody was going to have to lose.

"It was a good opportunity to beat a good team, and we were darn close." ■

Chiefs defensive back Bashaud Breeland (21) celebrates his 100-yard fumble recovery for a touchdown. PAUL SANCYA / AP PHOTO

INDIANAPOLIS 19, KANSAS CITY 13

OCTOBER 6, 2019 | KANSAS CITY, MISSOURI

Offensive Performance

Colts shut down Mahomes, Chiefs offense

The way Indianapolis handled the Kansas City Chiefs on Sunday night sent a jolt through the NFL, whether it was dominating the line of scrimmage or shutting down Patrick Mahomes and Co. on defense.

The one place the shock didn't reverberate? The visiting locker room in Arrowhead Stadium.

"The one emotion we were not feeling is shock. I can't even explain it," Colts coach Frank Reich said after the 19-13 victory. "The way guys were walking down the hallway, it was `We're not going to be denied. We have to get on track. We've got to do it.' I just knew it was real. I felt it all week.

"There was just an air of confidence and belief that we would do what we did today."

Marlon Mack ran for 132 yards, and ageless kicker Adam Vinatieri knocked through four field goals, as the Colts atoned ever-so-slightly for a January playoff defeat inside the same stadium.

Asked what the message was pregame, longtime Chiefs linebacker-turned-Colts defensive end Justin Houston replied: "To come out here and play our game. To leave it out there every snap, to play with your heart, play with your soul. And I think we did that tonight."

The Colts (3-2) allowed points on the Chiefs' first two possessions before shutting them out until Harrison Butker's field goal with 1:16 to go. Indianapolis recovered the onside kick without any issue and ran out the clock to celebrate a big win heading into its bye.

Mahomes threw for 321 yards and a touchdown, and the Chiefs (4-1) had just 36 yards rushing despite getting top running back Damien Williams back from an injury, all while watching their record streak of 22 straight games scoring at least 26 points come to a crashing conclusion.

"Penalties are really what hurt us today," said Chiefs coach Andy Reid, whose team was flagged 11 times for 125 yards. "You get things going, all of a sudden you're going backward, and it's tough in this league to do that against a good team and win."

In an air-it-out era of the NFL, the Colts also won by dominating the line of scrimmage.

On offense, their big line bruised a Kansas City defensive front that lost Chris Jones and Xavier Williams to injuries. On defense, the Colts spent most of the night in the Kansas City backfield, plugging up holes in the running game and relentlessly pressuring the reigning

Colts defensive tackle Grover Stewart (90) sacks Chiefs quarterback Patrick Mahomes (15) during the second half. REED HOFFMANN / AP PHOTO

league MVP on passing downs.

Mahomes was sacked four times and hit plenty more. At one point in the second half, Cam Erving was pushed so far into Mahomes' face that the backup left tackle stepped on his quarterback's ankle, leaving Mahomes to hobble to the sideline when Kansas City was forced to punt.

"In this league, the margin of error is tiny," said Mahomes, who dismissed the seriousness of his injury. "If you're not executing at a high level you're going to lose."

The Colts and Chiefs mostly played to a first-half stalemate, but the second of Vinatieri's four field goals made it 13-10 at the break. The Chiefs' prolific offense continued to sputter in the second half, and the Colts essentially played a game of keep-away throughout the third quarter and into the fourth.

"You don't need a large playbook to convert third-and-1," Chiefs defensive end Frank Clark said. ∎

Chiefs defensive back Tyrann Mathieu heads upfield after intercepting a second quarter pass. G. NEWMAN LOWRANCE / AP PHOTO

The Cheetah
Hill a headache for opposing defenses

After the Kansas City Chiefs' Week 9 win over the Minnesota Vikings, all the buzz seemed to surround wide receiver Tyreek Hill sprinting down the field to catch up to – and pass – teammate Damien Williams on Williams' 91-yard touchdown run.

According to NFL Next Gen Stats data, Hill hit a top speed of 22.64 mph on the play, the fastest speed by a wide receiver this year.

While impressive, it was one of the least important things Hill did that day. Hill had multiple remarkable moments, including when he caught a 41-yard pass late by tracking it better than cornerback Trae Waynes and then outmuscling his defender to make the catch.

"He would have been a great center fielder," Chiefs coach Andy Reid said of Hill's unusual ability to follow the ball down the field. "He's got a unique combination [of skills].

"The thing that amazes me the most is he's fast and quick, but it's his endurance being fast and quick. Normally you don't see that. I tell him he's got this 'Cheetah' nickname but he's really not a cheetah. They've got a burst and they go rest for about eight hours. That's not this guy. He can keep going over and over again. It's pretty amazing."

Hill's speed is what generates a lot of attention and it's a major reason for his big-play ability. But his other qualities -- a rare ability to track deep passes and a vertical jump that allows him to high-point throws -- are just as important for the 5-foot-10 Hill to outmaneuver bigger defensive backs.

"There aren't many guys out there like him," Chiefs backup quarterback Matt Moore said. "I've played with some good ones, but he's different. To know he can track down any ball and use his speed and his talents to get open the way he does, it's a nice feeling knowing you've got him out there."

Chiefs safety Tyrann Mathieu has never played against Hill in a game, only in practice this season as a teammate. But Mathieu was moved after the Vikings game to tweet about Hill's collection of skills.

"Most players are competitive, but he has competitive greatness," Mathieu said recently in explanation. "What I mean by that is in tough situations, critical moments, only a few people can make certain plays. He's one of those players.

"The only way you can cover him is to have that competitive greatness yourself. You have to know the ball is coming to him and in your mind you believe you can make the play. You just have to match his energy, his attitude and that's hard to do. He's on another level most of the time."

This is high praise from Mathieu, who at various points in his career has been a teammate of Odell Beckham Jr., Larry Fitzgerald and DeAndre Hopkins.

"Those guys can catch most balls, but I've never seen anybody do it like [Hill] being that size," Mathieu said.

Chiefs defensive coordinator Steve Spagnuolo was with the New York Giants in 2017 when he coached against Hill. He recalled it being a dilemma preparing a plan for Hill and not just because he's fast.

"I don't know if I've seen anybody attacking the football better than he does and he forces a defense to become simpler," Spagnuolo said. "Part of that is, a) because of his abilities and, b) because of what Andy and [offensive coordinator Eric Bieniemy] do with him, how much they move him around. He's always in motion. That creates some headaches. Teams that might want to play man coverage might want to think twice about that."

Hill is one of five players in NFL history with 20 or more 40-yard touchdowns at age 25 or younger, alongside Hall of Famers Bob Hayes,

Randy Moss, Gale Sayers and Lance Alworth. Despite missing four games early in the season because of an injury, Hill has eight catches of at least 20 yards this season, including five in the past two games. And again, it's not all about speed. In his first game back from the injury, Hill made a leaping 46-yard catch on which NFL NextGen stats measured him with a 40.5-inch vertical.

Hill shrugged at the mention of most of these plays, though he did make fun of the notion it appeared at first that Moore threw the ball too far on his touchdown catch against Minnesota.

"Can't nobody overthrow me," Hill said.

Patrick Mahomes did overthrow him during the Chief's Week 10 loss to the Tennessee Titans – a game in which Hill had 157 receiving yards on a career-best 11 catches – but it's an unusual event. Hill played well during his time with Moore at quarterback, but having a player with Mahomes' abilities makes Hill even more effective.

"Just do the math," Spagnuolo said. "You'd like to spy somebody on the quarterback and you'd like to double [Hill]. So you start adding it up and who's left to cover all the other receivers?

"That's why I say defenses need to become simpler because of him." ■

HOUSTON 31, KANSAS CITY 24

OCTOBER 13, 2019 | KANSAS CITY, MISSOURI

Texas Trouble

Watson, Hyde lead Texans past Chiefs

There were plenty of people standing on the Houston Texans sideline that felt they had something to prove against the Kansas City Chiefs on Sunday.

Just about all of them succeeded, too.

Deshaun Watson threw for 280 yards and a touchdown while running for two more, outdueling Chiefs counterpart Patrick Mahomes, who was famously picked two spots ahead of him in the 2017 draft.

Carlos Hyde ran for 116 yards and a touchdown against the team that traded him to Houston in the preseason, when the Chiefs decided there was no room for him in their own backfield.

Most importantly, Bill O'Brien proved he could beat a team pegged a Super Bowl contender, leading the Texans to a come-from-behind 31-24 victory after losing three of his last four to Kansas City.

"They care about the team. They seem to have fun with each other. We've just got to keep it going," said O'Brien, whose losses to the Chiefs include a postseason defeat. "We just had a really good win against a good team, but we're 4-2 and 4-2 gets you nowhere."

Better than being 3-3, though.

That was still a possibility until DeAndre Hopkins made a sliding grab on fourth-and-3 from the Kansas City 27 with just under 2 minutes to go. That allowed the Texans to run out the clock and deal the Chiefs (4-2) their second consecutive loss—both at Arrowhead Stadium.

Mahomes, hobbled once again by a sore left ankle, finished with 273 yards passing and three TDs while throwing his first interception of the season. Two of the scores went to Tyreek Hill, who returned for the first time since breaking his collarbone in a Week 1 win in Jacksonville.

The first pick Mahomes had thrown this season was nearly wiped out when an official threw a flag for pass interference. But after referee Shawn Hochuli announced the penalty, the officials huddled and decided to pick up the flag in a bizarre series of events.

"It was man coverage and I saw (Travis) Kelce getting ready to do his move, so I threw it to where he was going to be and he got tackled," Mahomes said. "With how the ruling worked, they said since the ball was uncatchable it wasn't pass interference."

"We just have to flip a few things," Chiefs

Chiefs tight end Travis Kelce (87) runs after the catch during the first half. GREG TROTT / AP PHOTO

Chiefs offensive linemen wait for center Austin Reiter (62) to snap the ball. GREG TROTT / AP PHOTO

ABOVE: Chiefs head coach Andy Reid argues a call with referee Shawn Hochuli (83) during the first half. COLIN E. BRALEY / AP PHOTO

RIGHT: Chiefs defensive back Tyrann Mathieu (32) pumps his fist in the air after sacking Houston quarterback DeShaun Watson (4). GREG TROTT / AP PHOTO

coach Andy Reid said. "The margin of winning and losing in this league is minute. We were this close to coming out of this thing with a win."

It wasn't a pretty game for either side. They combined for 21 penalties totaling nearly 150 yards, and that didn't include close to a dozen flags that were offsetting, overruled or declined.

It was Kansas City that started hot, engineering drives of at least 90 yards twice in the first quarter. Hill finished the first with a 46-yard reception – the first touchdown throw in a first quarter by Mahomes since Week 1 – while Damien Williams finished the second with a 14-yard TD catch.

In between, Hyde coughed up the ball on Houston's first offensive play.

But the big running back soon atoned for his mistake. Hyde battered the Chiefs' porous run defense the rest of the game, punctuating a big first half against his ex-team with a short touchdown run.

"We haven't played a perfect game on defense," Chiefs defensive end Frank Clark said, "and we're not going to play a perfect game, but we need to play a bit better. We need to eliminate the rush. When you eliminate the rush, you can have more fun." ∎

KANSAS CITY 30, DENVER 6
OCTOBER 17, 2019 | DENVER, COLORADO

Back on Track
Mahomes hurt as Chiefs crush Broncos

The Kansas City Chiefs rediscovered their mojo but lost their maestro.

The Chiefs rallied around their fallen superstar and snapped a two-game skid with a 30-6 thrashing of the Denver Broncos on Thursday night after reigning MVP Patrick Mahomes dislocated his right knee in a pileup near the goal line in the first half.

"I've never seen anything like that on the field before," Denver defensive end Shelby Harris said. "His knee was literally all the way to the side, his kneecap was. You never want to see anyone get hurt, especially like that. I hope everything is good and I hope he has a speedy recovery."

Chiefs coach Andy Reid said after the game that didn't know how serious Mahomes' injury was, but added that, "We're good with whatever direction this thing goes."

Backup Matt Moore threw a 57-yard touchdown pass to Tyreek Hill and the Chiefs (5-2) collected nine sacks, gave up a season-low 71 yards rushing and beat the Broncos (2-5) for the eighth straight time.

His balky left ankle heavily taped, Mahomes completed 10 of 11 passes for 76 yards and a touchdown, before getting injured on a successful sneak on fourth-and-inches at the Denver 5 early in the second quarter.

One by one, players peeled off the pile but when Mahomes didn't get up, the stadium grew quiet, Broncos players knelt and some Chiefs stormed away in aguish as their quarterback ripped off his helmet and covered his face.

Broncos cornerback Chris Harris Jr. went over to shake Mahomes' hand as he awaited medical help, his right knee stuck in an awkward angle.

"Hopefully he's not too injured, for the season," Harris said. "He's great for our league, he's a great player. So, hopefully he's not hurt too bad."

As players milled about nervously, the Chiefs' medical personnel appeared to pop Mahomes' right knee back in place before he was helped from the field and taken into the locker room.

"Excited for the win," Moore said. "At the same time, a guy like Patrick goes down it can be deflating."

Before he got hurt, Mahomes became the fastest player in NFL history to throw for 7,500 yards, in just his 25th game.

Mahomes, who has 15 TDs and one

Chiefs quarterback Patrick Mahomes (15) is helped off the field after getting injured during the first half. ERIC BAKKE / AP PHOTO

interception this season, didn't speak with reporters after the game but he did lead the team's "breakdown," in the winning locker room, praising Moore, who completed 10 of 19 passes for 117 yards, and the defense.

"Just seeing him in the locker room after the game, standing on his feet and just super optimistic about everything I think that shows one more time how strong of a man he is and how good of leader he is," said guard Laurent Duvernay-Tardif. "He's said, `I'm going to get better, we're going to get this team back on track,' and it was great to just see him walk and smile at the end."

The Broncos had won two straight and were aiming to turn the AFC West upside down by handling the Chiefs their third straight loss. But the Chiefs, who were 24th in the league with just 11 sacks coming in, sacked Flacco a career-high eight times and held Denver's running back duo in check after allowing an average of 190 over their previous four games. ∎

Chiefs quarterback Matt Moore (8) replaced the injured Mahomes and went 10-19 for 117 yards with one touchdown.
JACK DEMPSEY / AP PHOTO

GREEN BAY 31, KANSAS CITY 24

OCTOBER 27, 2019 | KANSAS CITY, MISSOURI

A Pack Attack

Rodgers, Jones too much for Chiefs

It was supposed to be a prime-time showdown between the Green Bay Packers and Kansas City Chiefs, division leaders each led by two of the most talented and exciting quarterbacks in the NFL.

Aaron Rodgers and the Packers lived up to the billing.

Patrick Mahomes never got the chance.

Rodgers threw for 305 yards and three touchdowns, two of them to Aaron Jones on a big night for the Green Bay running back, and the Packers held off fill-in quarterback Matt Moore and the rest of the banged-up Chiefs for a 31-24 victory Sunday night.

"I totally trust our quarterback," Packers coach Matt LaFleur said, "and I trust Aaron Jones as a receiver. He made some great plays all night long."

Jones, who briefly left with a shoulder injury, had seven catches for 159 yards and added 67 on the ground – a big chunk of them in the closing minutes, when the Packers (7-1) sealed their first win at Arrowhead Stadium since Nov. 4, 2007.

The Chiefs (5-3) hoped Mahomes could make a miraculous recovery 10 days after dislocating his kneecap in Denver in time to play. But after the league MVP was limited all week in practice, coach Andy Reid announced Friday his franchise quarterback would be inactive for the game.

Moore took the reins of the high-powered offense and fared well, throwing for 267 yards with two touchdowns and no picks in the ex-high school coach's first start in more than two years.

It wasn't the Rodgers-Mahomes matchup everyone wanted, but Moore and Co. made sure it was still an entertaining game between teams with Super Bowl aspirations.

It started like most outside the walls of 1 Arrowhead Drive expected, with Rodgers slicing up the defense and Green Bay marching for two quick touchdowns.

But after a shaky start by Moore, the journeyman quarterback found a groove. He led the Chiefs on an 89-yard drive that ended with a make-it-rain 29-yard touchdown pass to Travis Kelce, then found Mecole Hardman on a 30-yard pitch-and-catch to knot the game.

The Chiefs led 17-14 at halftime, raising some eyebrows across the league.

"Once we got in the flow," Moore said, "we were kind of rolling for a little while."

Chiefs tight end Travis Kelce (87) celebrates with a pose after scoring in the second quarter. ED ZURGA / AP PHOTO

LaFleur made a couple adjustments, though, and Rodgers and Co. began to move the ball once more. They used a 15-play drive that soaked up more than half the third quarter to get a tying field goal, then got the ball back when LeSean McCoy fumbled on the very next play.

Five players later, Rodgers conjured up more of his magic.

With third down at the 3, he dropped back and was flushed from the pocket. He rolled to his right and threw a blind pass to the back corner of the end zone, where Damien Williams somehow took the ball away from Chiefs linebacker Ben Niemann while tapping both feet inbounds.

Rodgers was lying flat on his back, staring at the sky, as the official signaled touchdown.

"I truly believe he was throwing it away," Chiefs safety Tyrann Mathieu said.

The Chiefs answered with another long drive, and just when it appeared they had finally been stopped, the Packers' Tramon Williams was flagged for illegal use of hands. That gave Kansas City the ball inside the 5, and Damien Williams scored on the next play to tie it again.

"We played hard and aggressive," Reid said, "but you know? When two good teams play each other, sometimes a turnover here or there can affect you and that's a little bit what happened tonight. But we can all do better, starting with me and my guys." ■

Packers running back Jamaal Williams (30) is drilled by Chiefs linebacker Reggie Ragland (59) on a second half carry. ED ZURGA / AP PHOTO

The Glue Guy

All-Pro Mathieu sets the tone for Chiefs D

Many of his teammates were busy celebrating a crucial Week 13 victory over the Oakland Raiders that in effect locked up a fourth straight AFC West championship for the Kansas City Chiefs, but safety Tyrann Mathieu was in his corner of the locker room looking ahead.

Sounding more like a coach than a player, Mathieu sized up an even bigger game and a meatier opponent in the Chiefs' Week 14 matchup with the New England Patriots.

"This week of practice will really be about discipline, assignment discipline, technique discipline because that's what the Patriots are going to do," Mathieu said. "They're going to run the ball, they're going to throw screens, they're going to wait for you to get out of your gap, they're going to wait for a deep safety to not be deep.

"It starts with me this week in practice, getting our guys ready, setting the tempo early in the week, letting them know we've got a big game this week."

Mathieu did it well enough that the Chiefs were able to do something they couldn't do in two tries without him last season: They beat the Patriots, a win that gave them a tiebreaker over New England and, when everything fell into place in Week 17, a first-round playoff bye.

The Chiefs had high expectations for Mathieu, 27, after acquiring him in free agency this offseason. They signed him to a three-year, $42 million contract, after he had played a season with the Houston Texans.

He met those expectations, earning first-team All-Pro at defensive back and second team as a safety.

The Chiefs knew from his past stops in Arizona and Houston that he would be someone others in the locker room would look and listen to in good times and bad. But they weren't quite expecting Mathieu to come in and take over the way he has in Year 1. Coach Andy Reid called the phenomenon extraordinary.

"This organization was blessed to have Eric Berry ... a great leader, tough, all those things," Reid said. "Before that I was with Brian Dawkins. I've been lucky to be around some really good safeties. They're all different in their own way but they're all great football players with great instincts and good leaders. They lead a different way.

"This kid here, he's a special kid. He's not the biggest guy. You're not looking at one of those huge safeties but, man, is he a good football player. He just gets it."

Mathieu walked into a Chiefs locker room that had lost some of its veteran defensive players and longtime voices in Berry and linebacker Justin Houston.

"I truly feel like they brought me here, obviously, to make plays, but to kind of set the tempo and set the energy in the building," Mathieu said. "I've always been a team guy. I feel I can go into any locker room and fit in for the most part, really relate to the most of the guys in the locker room. That's all I tried to do here is come in, play my role, be a veteran and be a leader on the defensive side and just try my best to kind of bring the team together and keep the team together whether things are going good or bad.

"The first thing with leadership is you have to understand your surroundings, your environment and the kind of people you're dealing with day to day. Here we had such a young team, such a vibrant team with a lot of different personalities. I've just tried to be myself."

One of his first gestures after signing with the Chiefs was small but telling: Mathieu was the first player to greet the team's other major offseason acquisition, defensive end Frank Clark, after he arrived in a trade with Seattle.

During offseason practice and training camp, Mathieu solidified himself as the defensive leader.

"He's the glue," defensive coordinator Steve Spagnuolo said. "He's the guy that can get in the huddle in practice and say, 'Hey, we need to step it up.' You need guys like that. That stuff, I value as a

coordinator. It makes my job a lot easier."

Spagnuolo relayed a conversation he had with an old friend who had coached Mathieu before the seventh-year safety signed with the Chiefs.

"He said something to the effect, 'He changed the building the minute he walked through the door,'" Spagnuolo said. "It just stuck with me as we evaluated the process.

"That kind of rang true. That's the kind of guy he is. He's dynamic, has a lot of energy. Guys gravitate to him. He's serious about what he's doing. When you're a coach and you have a player like that, that helps."

Mathieu immediately became the player the Chiefs gather around at the end of their pregame warm-up, an honor usually reserved for someone who has been with the team for some years.

"Everything that he does and everything he that he says, he speaks it into existence," Clark said. "I love hearing him speak to us on Sundays because it's a different type of motivation. He's going to bring the best out of everyone around him, whether you're a first-year guy, a fifth-year guy, a Pro Bowler, an All-Pro, Super Bowl-winning quarterback. ... He's a motivator.

"It's not just about him being on defense. He's going to motivate the whole team. I'm sure he's motivating QB1 [Patrick Mahomes]. I'm sure he's motivating the Cheetah [Tyreek Hill]. I'm sure he's motivating the coaches to coach better."

He's also a teacher. Mathieu had a role in the development of rookie safety Juan Thornhill, whose season ended when he tore his ACL in the final regular-season game against the Los Angeles Chargers but showed promise up to that point.

"He just told me to be myself," said Thornhill, who had three interceptions this season and returned one for a touchdown in the December win against the Raiders. "When you be yourself, you make more plays. I'm just going out there and having fun and that's probably the biggest tip he's given me all year.

"The guy is a heck of a player. I wouldn't be where I am now if it wasn't for him. He's always

giving me little, small tips that help me become a better player. He's taught me a lot."

On the field, the Chiefs have asked much of Mathieu. He lined up as a slot cornerback on 411 snaps, safety 359 and linebacker 224 times. He wound up leading the Chiefs with four interceptions.

"He wears a lot of hats," defensive backs coach Sam Madison said. "Early in the year, we just wanted to put guys in situations to be comfortable. He understands the defense. ... Since he's been at LSU, he's played all over the place. It was just a natural fit for him. He's taken to it very well. I talked to him a few weeks ago, telling him just to be patient and try not to go out there and find the plays [but] let them come to him. That's what he's been doing."

Asked whether the Chiefs were concerned about overloading Mathieu, Madison said: "We thought about it. But when that kid comes into the meeting rooms, he has all the answers that we ask. When we threw him out there, it doesn't really seem to bother him. We knew all the different positions that he played previously [and] we're just trying to apply it to what we have. He wants to be out there. He loves football. When you have players like that, you try to give them as much as possible to see what sticks and what falls by the wayside. A lot of this stuff is sticking."

Mathieu was once one of the fastest players on the field. He was a top punt returner earlier in his career. But after having two serious knee injuries, he said he's not the same player he once was athletically.

But he's having a bigger impact for a team that needed it – the Chiefs have allowed an NFL-best 11.5 points per game since Week 11 a season after struggling – on and off the field.

"I've grown," Mathieu said. "I'm in my seventh year now and it's bigger than me. It's about me playing well but getting other people around me to play well.

"One of the best decisions I made was coming here. It's been going well." ■

KANSAS CITY 26, MINNESOTA 23
NOVEMBER 3, 2019 | KANSAS CITY, MISSOURI

Kickin' Into Gear
Butker's late FGs help Chiefs rally past Vikings

Harrison Butker watched his 44-yard field goal split the uprights, the clocks inside Arrowhead Stadium reading zero, and the Chiefs kicker turned and sprinted the other way in celebration.

The first person to join him? Patrick Mahomes.

The reigning league MVP, who missed his second straight game while recovering from a dislocated kneecap, looked just fine as he joined Butker and the rest of his Kansas City teammates in a midfield mob after their heart-stopping 26-23 victory over the Minnesota Vikings on Sunday.

"I was sprinting down, maybe just from my soccer background growing up – that's what you do when you score," said Butker, who thought the winner may have been tipped. "When I was going I saw Patrick, and I wanted to embrace him and I'm like, `Nah, he can't get hurt."

Matt Moore started in Mahomes' place and threw for 275 yards and a touchdown, and he made the crucial plays when they mattered. He hit favorite target Tyreek Hill to convert a key third down and set up Butker's career best-tying 54-yard field goal to knot the game, then found Hill again a couple minutes later to make the winner a little more manageable.

"I thought, Matt, that was a gutsy performance by him," said Chiefs coach Andy Reid, whose team snapped a three-game skid at Arrowhead Stadium. "He took a couple of licks there and he got back up and finished. But just him calming the storm I thought was good."

Hill finished with six catches for 140 yards for the Chiefs (6-3), including a spectacular TD grab, while Damien Williams ran for 125 yards – most of it on a 91-yard touchdown run.

Kirk Cousins threw for 220 yards and three touchdowns for the Vikings (6-3), though he struggled to deal with the Chiefs' blitzes late in the game. Dalvin Cook was held to 71 yards rushing while top wide receiver Stefon Diggs had a single catch for four yards.

The Chiefs largely controlled the first half, building a 10-7 lead with the ball in the closing minutes. But they proceeded to go three-and-out, the Vikings marched downfield for a tying field goal, then got the ball back when Mecole Hardman fumbled the opening kickoff of the second half.

Suddenly, it was the Vikings who had taken control.

Chiefs kicker Harrison Butker (7) celebrates his game-winning field goal. COLIN E. BRALEY / AP PHOTO

ABOVE: Chiefs wide receiver Tyreek Hill (10) climbs the wall and sits with fans after he scoring on a 40-yard touchdown reception. COLIN E. BRALEY / AP PHOTO

RIGHT: Hill (10) makes a 41-yard catch against Vikings cornerback Trae Waynes (26) during the second half. REED HOFFMANN / AP PHOTO

They needed just five plays to punch it into the end zone, despite a holding penalty setting them back. Amir Abdullah finished it with a 17-yard catch in which nobody was within 10 yards of him.

Hardman hurt the Chiefs again by failing to call a fair catch on a punt downed at their 3. But that flub was rendered irrelevant when Williams took a handoff, found a gaping hole on the left side of the line and made the only safety in front of him miss on a 91-yard touchdown run.

Minnesota answered in the seesaw affair.

Leaning heavily on Cook, the league's leading rusher, the Vikings marched 75 yards without facing third down until the final play. That's when Cousins hit Kyle Rudolph from 3 yards out for the score, taking advantage of a Kansas City defense with just 10 players on the field.

After trading punts, the Chiefs put together another drive. Moore hit Hill to convert a key third down, and Butker matched his career long with a 54-yard field goal with 2:30 to go.

It was a monumental kick – and he had another coming a couple minutes later.

"This was a great win, a great team win," Hill said. "We all did our thing, and this team needed this victory because the vibe in the locker room the last few weeks has been down." ∎

TENNESSEE 35, KANSAS CITY 32
NOVEMBER 10, 2019 | NASHVILLE, TENNESSEE

A Spoiled Return
Titans rally to spoil Mahomes' return

Forcing Patrick Mahomes and the Kansas City Chiefs to settle for a bunch of field goals gave the Tennessee Titans a chance to stay close.

Ryan Tannehill and a cornerback only activated off injured reserve a week ago helped make the Chiefs pay for their fifth and sixth attempts.

Tannehill threw a 23-yard touchdown to Adam Humphries with 23 seconds left, and Joshua Kalu blocked a last-second field goal attempt to beat the Chiefs 35-32 to spoil the return of NFL MVP Patrick Mahomes.

"It's fun to win a game like that, battle back in the fourth-quarter at home and find a way to win is a ton of fun," Tannehill said.

The Titans (5-5) only had a chance after a bad snap by the Chiefs on Harrison Butker's fifth field goal attempt of the day. Kansas City coach Andy Reid blamed communication for the snap taking holder Dustin Colquitt by surprise, and he threw the ball away in desperation for an intentional grounding call, setting the Titans up at their own 39.

Tannehill scrambled for 18, hit Anthony Firsker for 20 yards and then found Humphries who ran in for the TD. Tannehill also ran for the 2-point conversion for a 35-32 lead.

The Chiefs (6-4) had a final chance with Mahomes. He drove them down, setting up Butker for another field goal try from 52 yards.

Kalu blocked the kick with his left hand, and the Titans ran onto the field to celebrate. Kalu wound up at the bottom of a pile, and he said he kept getting closer each time watching the Chiefs' cadence, hands and eyes. The block was a blur but not his decision to jump at the snap.

"As soon as I hit it, it was automatic joy," said Kalu, recently activated from injured reserve.

Kansas City coach Andy Reid, now 1-8 all-time against Tennessee, said he wanted to see a replay of the blocked field goal thinking Kalu was offside. But Reid took the blame for the loss.

"We were in position to close it, and we didn't get that done," Reid said. "My responsibility. Then we were too sloppy."

Derrick Henry ran for 188 yards, including a 68-yard TD that put Tennessee up 20-19 with 5:58 left in the third. His 1-yard TD with 6:26 remaining pulled the Titans within 29-27.

Tannehill finished with 181 yards passing and ran for 37 yards for the win.

The loss spoiled the best passing game this season for Mahomes as the Chiefs

Chiefs wide receiver Mecole Hardman (17) takes off for the end zone on a 63-yard touchdown reception. JAMES KENNEY / AP PHOTO

outgained the Titans 530-371. Mahomes threw for 446 yards and three touchdowns. His best play came with the pocket collapsing around him when he jumped up to throw over the linemen to Mecole Hardman who ran for a 63-yard TD with 11:54 left and a 29-20 lead.

"The knee feels fine, and I'm glad to get through another game," Mahomes said of his knee and ankle that had been hurting last month.

Mahomes looked very healthy playing for the first time since dislocating his right kneecap Oct. 17. He got lucky when his first pass first ruled an interception was overturned by replay for Titans safety Kenny Vaccaro trapping the ball on the ground. Mahomes capped the Chiefs' first drive with a 3-yard shovel pass to Travis Kelce.

The Chiefs sacked Tannehill four times and also forced a fumble but could only turn that into one of Butker's four made field goals. ∎

Titans defensive back Joshua Kalu (46) blocks a 52-yard field goal attempt by Chiefs kicker Harrison Butker (7) on the final play.
MARK ZALESKI / AP PHOTO

KANSAS CITY 24, L.A. CHARGERS 17
NOVEMBER 18, 2019 | ESTADIO AZTECA, MEXICO CITY

Successful Road Trip

Mahomes, Chiefs get just enough offense in Mexico City

Nearly everything about this Monday night game felt foreign to Patrick Mahomes and the Kansas City Chiefs, from the gasp-inducing altitude of raucous Azteca Stadium to the struggles of their powerhouse offense.

Mahomes loved the experience, but didn't love how his offense played. The Chiefs' defense picked it up time and again, culminating in the final pick that sent them all back home as winners.

"We kept that confidence all game long," Mahomes said. "We knew that someone was going to make a play to win the game."

Daniel Sorensen snared Philip Rivers' fourth interception at the goal line with 18 seconds to play, and the Chiefs stayed on top of the AFC West with a 24-17 victory over the Los Angeles Chargers.

Mahomes passed for 182 yards and hit Travis Kelce for his only touchdown, while LeSean McCoy and Darrel Williams rushed for touchdowns as the Chiefs (7-4) hung on to win the fourth regular-season NFL game played in Mexico despite being held to 310 yards of offense. They also survived a few problems with Azteca's grass field and a one-sided first half favoring the Chargers (4-7), who racked up 312 yards without a touchdown.

The Chargers had the ball six times over the first two quarters and advanced into Kansas City territory on five of those possessions. They ran 20 plays from scrimmage on the Chiefs' side of the field.

And they still failed to reach the end zone, continuing a season-long struggle to score points.

After throwing his second interception of the season in the first half, Mahomes led two sharp scoring drives in the third quarter with help from Kelce, who caught seven passes for 92 yards. Mahomes also led the Chiefs with 59 yards rushing while his defense – which had only six interceptions all season coming into Mexico City – held Los Angeles to eight points in the second half.

But the win still wasn't assured until Sorensen grabbed Rivers' underthrown pass to Austin Ekeler at the goal line to secure the Chiefs' 10th win over Los Angeles in 11 meetings.

"I was real proud of our defense for the job that they did," Chiefs coach Andy Reid said.

Chiefs tight end Travis Kelce (87), right, celebrates with teammate Demarcus Robinson (11) after scoring a touchdown in the third quarter.
REBECCA BLACKWELL / AP PHOTO

Chiefs running back Darrel Williams scores on a 6-yard touchdown run. REBECCA BLACKWELL / AP PHOTO

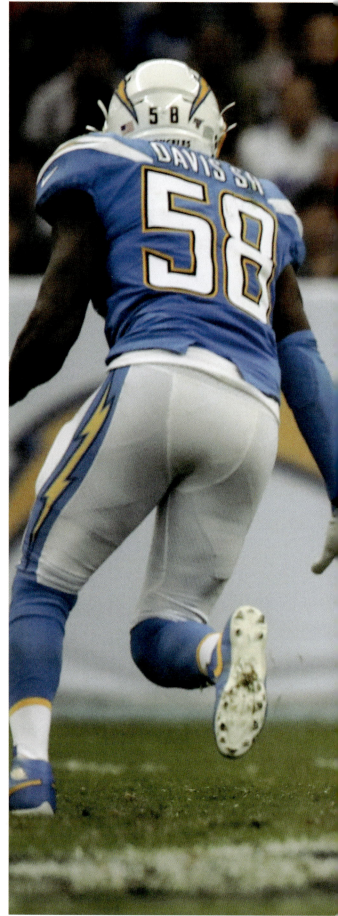

"Four takeaways, so for the guys that intercepted the football and then helped create the turnovers, I'm proud of those guys."

Rivers passed for 353 yards during his first four-interception game since November 2016 for the Chargers, whose playoff hopes are nearly dead after five losses in seven games.

One year after the NFL called off a game at Azteca Stadium on short notice because of poor field conditions, these teams played an entertaining game in the 7,200-foot elevation and on the Azteca grass, which yielded several significant divots from sharp stops or changes of direction.

The Rams and Chiefs were scheduled to play here last season, but severe damage to the turf field compelled the NFL to relocate the game to Los Angeles on six days' notice.

Tyreek Hill left the field with a right hamstring injury after the Chiefs' second offensive series, although it didn't appear to be caused by the turf. The speedster watched the second half from the sideline. ■

ABOVE: A general view of Estadio Azteca prior to the game. BEN LIEBENBERG / AP PHOTO

RIGHT: Chiefs quarterback Patrick Mahomes (15) tries to scramble away from Chargers linebacker Thomas Davis (58). BEN LIEBENBERG / AP PHOTO

Reid Gets Another Shot at Super Bowl

Andy Reid is headed back to the Super Bowl for the first time since the 2004 season, and it sounds as if he'll have legions of supporters following him.

Reid's Kansas City Chiefs did what they couldn't do last January: get the job done. Kansas City overcame another early deficit to run away with a 35-24 win over the Tennessee Titans in the AFC Championship Game, securing the team's first berth in the sport's biggest game in 50 years a year after falling painfully short against New England.

There's a long list of those who are incredibly happy for him.

"It's everything," Chiefs general manager Brett Veach said of getting Reid back to the Super Bowl. "He's given, not just me, but so many people an opportunity in this league. When I first started out he believed in me and it motivates me to bust my tail every day and emulate his work ethic. It means the world. That's why we know we are not done yet. We have one more game to go."

The mustachioed coach who rose from Packers offensive assistant to Philadelphia Eagles head coach in 1999 had to wait a decade and a half to make a return trip to the place where his Eagles fell painfully short to the league's dynasty of this century. Few believed the 2004 run to Jacksonville would be the Eagles' last trip under Reid, and even though Philadelphia remained a contender for the majority of his time with the team, they never again quite got over the hump to play for the Lombardi during his tenure.

That led to Reid's parting with the Eagles at the end of the 2012 season, but he wasn't out of work for long. The Chiefs came calling, and seven years later, they're headed back to the Super Bowl for the first time since the 1969 season.

"Look, any time you are having a tough season, it is hard to envision playing in the Super Bowl, but things changed for us seven years ago when we were lucky enough to lure Andy Reid and his wife, Tammy, to Kansas City," Chiefs chairman and CEO Clark Hunt said. "It has been a building process ever since then. He came in day one and we started winning games. We reeled off nine straight wins for the start of the Andy Reid tenure here in Kanas City. He got us to the championship game last year.

"We really felt like going into the season that we had a great opportunity to get back and really the credit goes to Andy, his coaching staff, our entire football operations department and also Mark Donovan, our president and his great staff. Those three groups really work well together, and we are fortunate because not every NFL team is like that, but we have three great leaders running our franchise and the three of them really deserve the credit for getting us here today."

It's a little special, too, because the AFC championship named after Chiefs founder Lamar Hunt now resides in Kansas City. The reality didn't seem like a possibility back in early 2013 when Hunt's son, Clark, was in pursuit of Reid.

It is now a reality, though, thanks to Reid's Chiefs, who embody their coach with their never-say-die attitude.

"Listen, first of all, I'm so happy for the Hunt

Family and bringing that trophy back here. Wow," Reid said. "How great is that, (cheering) that's right. I'm proud of our team for the effort they showed today. 'Never die' is kind of their thing. I mean getting behind like this is tough on an old guy, but they did a nice job coming back.

"Again, fired up. Fired up to go to Miami. I need to get on a diet so I can fit in my clothes and we can go do our thing. Very proud, very proud of everybody and the job that they did. The coaches, the coordinators for the plan that they had. EB (offensive coordinator Eric Bieniemy) talked to the team last night and got them all fired up. EB's been there as a player and a coach. I thought he had some real great words for the players and coaches for that matter. The guys came out and played with a ton of energy. They had a few ups and downs there early. We were able to overcome those and get ourselves going in the right direction. Anyways. The fans were phenomenal. That thing out there right now, unbelievable. It was very good."

Reid's Chiefs are filled with players who have remained hungry for a chance to play for the most important trophy in American sports. Safety Tyrann Mathieu, for one, had to make it to his third team in seven seasons for a chance to contend for a conference title. Thanks to the contributions of he and many others in red and white, Kansas City – a participant in the game's first Super Bowl way back in January 1967 – is back on the game's biggest stage during the league's 100th season.

Even in a moment of football-driven euphoria, Mathieu was thinking about the sideline-patrolling leader of his team.

"I'm so happy for Coach Reid," Mathieu said. "I say it all the time, but you think about his coaching tree. You think about all of the guys that he's made into head coaches. A lot of guys that he's really given opportunities to, especially minorities. You think about the players that have come up under him and their Hall of Fame-caliber. I think he's a great coach and he's all about his players and the team. Most importantly, he allows us to be ourselves. He's not restricting us from our personalities, and I think that has a lot to do with us fighting through adversity and believing in ourselves. That's committing to each other and playing hard week in and week out."

They'll have a chance to give their full effort for each other, and their 61-year-old coach, one last time in the same state in which Reid last reached the Super Bowl. We'll soon learn whether he can secure his second title – and first as a head coach – when the Chiefs face the San Francisco 49ers in Miami. ∎

Andy Reid gives Chiefs GM Brett Veach a hug after winning the AFC Championship Game. G. NEWMAN LOWRANCE / AP PHOTO

KANSAS CITY 40, OAKLAND 9
DECEMBER 1, 2019 | KANSAS CITY, MISSOURI

A Dominating Performance
Chiefs seize AFC West control

Patrick Mahomes looked up at the scoreboard late in the third quarter and was stunned to see the Kansas City Chiefs had taken a 31-0 lead over the AFC West rival Oakland Raiders.

"I felt like we'd only scored a couple of times," he said.

That's because the Chiefs' high-powered offense didn't need to do a whole lot Sunday.

Their defense and the inept Raiders took care of the rest.

Mahomes did throw for a touchdown and run for a touchdown, but it was Juan Thornhill's pick-6 and a long list of blunders by Derek Carr and Co. that really made the difference.

They allowed Kansas City to cruise to a 40-9 victory and into a two-game lead over the Raiders in the division race.

"That's what we expected all season long, and you've seen it week by week the defense getting better," Mahomes said, "and the offense just played in the flow of the game. We've been in every type of game so far and we've been finding ways to win them."

LeSean McCoy and Darwin Thompson also had TD runs for the Chiefs (8-4), who can clinch a fourth straight division title with a win over New England and an Oakland loss to Tennessee next weekend.

Oakland (6-6) sure didn't play like a team fighting for a piece of the division lead.

Carr dropped to 0-6 at Arrowhead Stadium with another miserable outing, throwing for 222 yards with a touchdown and two interceptions. The Raiders failed to score twice in the red zone, were penalized 12 times for 99 yards, and watched Kansas City put together a 9 1/2-minute drive almost entirely on the ground that soaked up most of the fourth quarter.

When the Raiders finally scored a touchdown in the last minute, the Chiefs blocked the extra point and returned it for two points – one more insult to Oakland in a game full of them.

Meanwhile, the Chiefs were not penalized once in a game for the first time since Dec. 8, 1974.

"Do that and be productive in the red zone," Chiefs coach Andy Reid said, "good things happen."

Both teams struggled to move the ball at times with frosty winds whipping at 40 mph out of the west. Flurries even fell during halftime, adding to the misery for fans huddled in the stands.

In the first half alone, Carr threw both of his interceptions; the Raiders lost a fumble

Chiefs quarterback Patrick Mahomes (15) scores on a 13-yard run. RYAN KING / AP PHOTO

ABOVE: Chiefs defensive back Rashad Fenton (27) celebrates with teammates Darron Lee (50) and Byron Pringle (13) after forcing a fumble. REED HOFFMANN / AP PHOTO

LEFT: Chiefs running back LeSean McCoy (25) stiff arms Raiders cornerback Trayvon Mullen (27) during a first half run. REED HOFFMANN / AP PHOTO

on a kick return; failed to convert on fourth-and-1; committed seven penalties; and watched Daniel Carlson yank a 44-yard field-goal attempt about 20 yards wide left.

The Chiefs took advantage of all the squandered opportunities.

Mahomes, who perhaps more than anyone benefited from a week off, capped a 47-yard drive in the first quarter with a short TD pass to Darrel Williams. Then, late in the first half, the reigning MVP scrambled to his left and ran untouched 13 yards for another touchdown.

The Chiefs put the game out of reach in the third quarter.

First, they moved swiftly downfield on the opening possession before Harrison Butker drilled a 50-yard field goal into the wind. Then, on their next possession, Mahomes threw a pick in the end zone that was overturned when replay showed wide receiver Demarcus Robinson was held on the play.

The penalty gave Kansas City the ball back and McCoy scored moments later.

"Every team that makes the playoffs, it's about what their defense can do. I think this week we were able to refocus," Chiefs safety Tyrann Mathieu said. "Our coaches did a good job of challenging us. Coming off the bye week, we knew what we needed to work on. I'm just proud of our guys. We haven't played well at home. This type of performance against a division team is pretty good." ■

KANSAS CITY 23, NEW ENGLAND 16

DECEMBER 8, 2019 | FOXBORO, MASSACHUSETTS

AFC West Champs
Chiefs survive mistakes to clinch division title

Patrick Mahomes got some help from the Chiefs defense to hold off the New England Patriots and wrap up the division title.

Kansas City clinched the AFC West when Bashaud Breeland knocked away Tom Brady's fourth-down pass attempt to Julian Edelman in the end zone and the Chiefs beat New England 23-16 on Sunday.

After building a 20-7 lead, the Chiefs survived a series of mistakes and questionable officiating to hold off a late rally by the defending Super Bowl champions.

Combined with Oakland's loss to Tennessee, the Chiefs (9-4) clinched the AFC West. The loss ended the Patriots' 21-game home win streak in the regular season and playoffs, which was tied for the longest in team history. It also was the third-longest string in NFL history.

Mahomes was 26 of 40 for 283 yards, a touchdown and interception, playing through a hand injury he suffered during Kansas City's second offensive series. Tight end Travis Kelce added a 4-yard TD run.

Mahomes now is the third quarterback this season to earn his first win against the Patriots, joining Baltimore's Lamar Jackson and Houston's Deshaun Watson. All three were previously 0-2.

"You want to beat the best. You want to go out and play against the best and give your best effort," Mahomes said. "It wasn't pretty the whole time. It was just a tough, hard-fought win.

He said he got creative after his injury.

"I let the trainers look at it. They gave me a good to go," Mahomes said. "I went out there, battled and figured out ways to throw the ball across the middle. Maybe not shoot those long shots I usually throw. But enough to get them back and still score touchdowns."

New England (10-3) has lost two in a row.

Tom Brady was under pressure all game and finished 19 of 36 for 169 yards, a touchdown and interception. the 169 yards are his second-fewest passing yards this season. He spoke after the game with his right elbow heavily wrapped.

"They threw a lot of different defenses at us," Brady said. "Some we handled well and some we didn't."

"It's tough trying to stop a guy like that with the weapons he's got," Chiefs linebacker Reggie Ragland said of Brady. "So, we just had

Chiefs quarterback Patrick Mahomes gets off the pass while in the grasp of Patriots defensive end John Simon. CHARLES KRUPA / AP PHOTO

Chiefs wide receiver Mecole Hardman (17), left, breaks away from the defense on his way to a 48-yard touchdown reception STEVEN SENNE / AP PHOTO

to do a good job of sound defense, let the offense do what they do. But if we keep playing defense like that, I thing we have a good shot of going where we want to go."

Trailing 23-16, New England got the ball back on its 32 with 5:04 to play. The Patriots immediately gained 35 yards on a pass from halfback James White to Jakobi Meyers to get into Kansas City territory. Officials appeared to miss a pass interference call on a deep pass to Phillip Dorsett and the Chiefs forced a fourth-and-6 at the 29.

But the 42-year-old Brady got free and scrambled 17 yards for a first down.

The Patriots couldn't get into the end zone, however, losing the rematch of January's AFC title game in Kansas City.

"Between last year and what was at stake this year," Chiefs defensive end Alex Okafor said, "to go into Foxborough and get this win, man, it was incredible."

Chiefs right tackle Mitchell Schwartz agreed but said the team still has some unfinished business ahead.

"There's still a while to go," Schwartz said. "Beating the Patriots in December isn't really the ultimate goal for the season. It's a good game for us, and obviously it puts us in a better position for the playoffs. It's just a good team win." ■

Chiefs tight end Travis Kelce (87) powers his way into the end zone for a first half touchdown. ELISE AMENDOLA / AP PHOTO

KANSAS CITY 23, DENVER 3
DECEMBER 15, 2019 | KANSAS CITY, MISSOURI

Snow Problem
Chiefs roll over Broncos at snowy Arrowhead

The Kansas City Chiefs turned Arrowhead Stadium into their own winter wonderland Sunday, mushing through the snow to an easy victory over the Denver Broncos as they march toward another postseason filled with possibilities.

Patrick Mahomes threw for 340 yards and two touchdowns, and Tyreek Hill and Travis Kelce were on the receiving end of many of his biggest throws, as the AFC West champions romped to a 23-3 victory over the rebuilding Broncos to remain in the hunt for the No. 2 playoff seed and a potential first-round bye.

"It was awesome. A lot of fun," said Mahomes, who showed no lingering effects from the hand his bruised last week. "The guys were embracing it. We knew it was going to snow. We practice in cold weather a lot. So you get there, you're already accustomed to it, and you go out there and play."

Like a bunch of kids getting a snow day from school, the Chiefs enjoyed every minute of it.

Hill caught five passes for 67 yards and both scores, and Kelce hauled in 11 catches for 142 yards to become the first tight end in NFL history with four consecutive 1,000-yard receiving seasons, helping the Chiefs (10-4) beat the Broncos for the ninth straight time. Denver (5-9) hasn't won in Kansas City since Sept. 17, 2015.

The Chiefs outscored their longtime division rival 53-9 this season.

"You just attack it. You can't let weather get into how you're playing the game or disrupt how you're playing the game," Kelce said. "That's the biggest thing in terms of mindset, going out there and not letting anything distract you."

Whether it was the weather or the suddenly stout Chiefs defense, the Broncos were so inept offensively that Kelce had more yards receiving at the start of the fourth quarter than they had total offense (139 yards). Phillip Lindsay was bottled up on the ground, and former Missouri standout Drew Lock – who grew up in the Kansas City suburb of Lee's Summit, Missouri – spent most of the day seeing red jerseys bearing down on him.

The rookie quarterback was 18 of 40 for 208 yards and an egregious interception in the end zone.

"I think he handled the conditions well. I didn't see him get flustered out there and

Chiefs wide receiver Tyreek Hill (10) makes a touchdown catch in front of Broncos cornerback Chris Harris Jr. during the first half. ED ZURGA / AP PHOTO

frustrated so that part was good," said Broncos coach Vic Fangio.

That was about the only good part. The Broncos finished with 251 yards, went 5 of 14 on third down and 1 of 3 on fourth, and were penalized seven times for 72 yards. They also went 0 for 2 in the red zone.

"When you play a team as good as the Chiefs," Fangio said, "you can't do that."

Flurries began to fall overnight, far earlier than meteorologists had predicted, and the intensifying snow caused major problems for people trying to get to the stadium. An hour before kickoff, dozens of workers were clearing off the yard lines, end zones and sidelines as the snow swirled inside the stadium. It really began to pick up again at halftime, obscuring Kauffman Stadium about a quarter mile away, and stadium workers flooded the field to clear what they could during every timeout.

"That was very fun," said Hill, who left the game after a couple of hard hits but returned to finish it out. "This is my first snow game and I had a blast with it. I don't want to do it again because it's very cold, but I had fun with it." ■

ABOVE: Chiefs receiver Sammy Watkins takes a moment to enjoy the snow.
REED HOFFMANN / AP PHOTO

RIGHT: Chiefs quarterback Patrick Mahomes (15) scrambles away from Broncos outside linebacker Von Miller (58) during the second half.
REED HOFFMANN / AP PHOTO

The Difference Maker

Mahomes has the spotlight all to himself

It wasn't that Patrick Mahomes slipped. Others just rose up to share the spotlight.

Lamar Jackson climbed higher, and faster, than most envisioned possible. Russell Wilson had never been better during a long, spectacular run that, eventually, will end in Canton, Ohio. Deshaun Watson's wizardry commanded attention. Kyler Murray served notice that he plans to be next on.center stage.

But not now.

Now, Mahomes is the last one standing, heading to the Super Bowl and, quite possibly, at the dawn of a new era in the NFL. Now, Mahomes is healthy and determined to take the step he fell short of last season. Now, we're reminded of whom this season was actually supposed to be about.

When the Kansas City Chiefs beat the Tennessee Titans in the AFC Championship Game, Mahomes became only the seventh African American passer in league history to lead a team to the Super Bowl.

Mahomes almost joined the list last season. But for the better part of two decades, Tom Brady has often ruined his counterparts' best-laid plans. With Brady and the New England Patriots no longer blocking his path, Mahomes took advantage — and with the smarts, heart, leadership and oh, so much arm talent — to finally guide the Chiefs back to a place they haven't been in 50 years. And Mahomes is laser focused on winning once there.

"It's an amazing accomplishment, first off, to win the AFC championship. I mean, at the beginning of the season, you have all these goals and it's a process," Mahomes said. "Obviously, it's exciting to play the AFC championship at home with the home fans. But now we're just going into the next one with the mentality of not coming up short."

Bad memories, at least in part, fueled the Chiefs' drive to their fourth consecutive AFC West title under head coach Andy Reid (the second straight with Mahomes atop the quarterback depth chart), the No. 2 overall seeding in the AFC playoffs and an historic 51-31 victory over the Houston Texans in the divisional round after they trailed by 24 points in the second quarter.

During one of the Chiefs' lowest moments against Houston, Mahomes' leadership skills were on full display. With Kansas City trailing 21-0 at the end of the first quarter, Mahomes gave an impassioned speech, encouraging his teammates to keep believing.

"I just wanted to make sure everyone was still in the right mindset. With everything that had happened at the beginning of the game, I still felt like we were doing good things, but we just weren't executing at a high enough level," Mahomes said. "I wanted to make sure I went to the guys and let them know that. It comes with knowing your teammates, knowing how the game's going, how to get back on it and back to where you need to be at."

In last season's AFC title game, the Chiefs lost on their home field to the Patriots in overtime 37-31. Mahomes never got the ball in that overtime, with Brady leading New England on a game-winning, 75-yard touchdown drive.

The loss was a crushing end to Mahomes' breakout season in his second year in the NFL and first as a starter. He produced eye-opening stats and played with flair en route to being

selected the Associated Press 2018 NFL MVP. Entering this season, the Chiefs were widely considered a top Super Bowl contender, and Mahomes was on the short list for the MVP award.

Then Jackson, superbly orchestrating an offense the Baltimore Ravens designed based on his skill set, skyrocketed to lead the league in touchdown passes, established a new NFL rushing record for quarterbacks and became the overwhelming MVP favorite. Wilson put the Seattle Seahawks on his shoulders, and Watson bailed out the Texans countless times. Meanwhile, Mahomes battled injuries, including a dislocated kneecap suffered in October that sidelined him for two games. Still, Kansas City led the AFC in passing yards and finished second in the conference in scoring. In the comeback against Houston, Mahomes was brilliant, passing for 321 yards and five touchdowns.

If the Chiefs defeat San Francisco to win the Super Bowl, Mahomes would join Doug Williams and Wilson as the only black passers to accomplish the feat. What's more, with Brady, 42, a free agent and the Patriots clearly in need of a major reboot on offense, the sun may have finally set on their dynasty.

Mahomes is only 24. Not to get too far ahead of things, but great quarterback play is the foundation of NFL dynasties. Barring the unforeseen, the Chiefs (who last reached the Super Bowl after the 1969 season) are positioned better than most at the game's most important position for the foreseeable future.

Former Pro Bowl signal-caller Donovan McNabb, who had a successful head coach-quarterback partnership with Reid with the Philadelphia Eagles, said he wouldn't be surprised if Reid and Mahomes appear in multiple Super Bowls together.

"We see how comfortable [Mahomes] is in [Reid's] offense, and how Andy's creating a great platform for him," said McNabb, a six-time Pro Bowler who led Philadelphia to seven postseason appearances and one Super Bowl appearance. "[Mahomes] is lightning in a bottle. … At any play, anytime, in a game, he'll throw a bomb that can kill you."

Mahomes is eligible for a contract extension in the offseason, and the Chiefs are expected to move quickly to lock up their franchise quarterback with a record-setting deal. Of course, that's a personnel matter for another day. At the moment, Mahomes is squarely focused on the ultimate team goal.

"Being in the Super Bowl, we're going to put the pressure on ourselves to find a way to win it," Mahomes said. "When you fall that short and that close last year, the next step is to get to the Super Bowl and then win it all." ∎

KANSAS CITY 26, CHICAGO 3

DECEMBER 22, 2019 | CHICAGO, ILLINOIS

Windy City Blowout

Mahomes throws 2 TDs, runs for 1 as Chiefs beat Bears

Patrick Mahomes kept the Kansas City Chiefs in the running for a first-round bye in the playoffs.

Mahomes outplayed Mitchell Trubisky, throwing for two touchdowns and running for another score, and the Chiefs beat the Chicago Bears 26-3 Sunday night for their fifth straight win.

Kansas City (11-4) remained a game behind New England for the AFC's second seed. The Patriots clinched their 11th consecutive AFC East championship by beating Buffalo on Saturday.

Mahomes' big game in his first appearance at Soldier Field is just another blow for Chicago in a rough season that began with Super Bowl hopes. The matchup between the Chiefs and Bears was billed as a Mahomes-Trubisky showdown. Mahomes' performance, though, reaffirmed which team got the better quarterback in the 2017 NFL Draft.

The Bears passed on Mahomes when they traded up a spot to grab Trubisky with the No. 2 overall pick. Mahomes went to Kansas City at No. 10 and won the MVP award last season.

Trubisky has not performed the way the Bears envisioned. And with their playoff hopes already dashed coming off an NFC North championship, they got outclassed by Kansas City.

"You know that there's a process to it and not everyone can be picked first," Mahomes said. "And I ended up in a great situation in Kansas City, a situation where I wanted to be at, an organization that's kind of taken me and made me the best player that I could be at this time. So I'm just excited that I'm here now and I was able to go out there and find a way to win the football game."

Mahomes, playing his 30th game, became the fastest player to reach the 9,000-yard passing mark. He was 23 of 33 for 251 yards, giving him 9,238 in three seasons. Hall of Famer Kurt Warner did it in 32 games.

Mahomes also has 75 touchdown passes, making him the fastest player to hit that mark.

"Patrick, obviously, had a nice day throwing it," Chiefs coach Andy Reid said. "He had some unbelievable throws in the mix there. Not a lot of guys can make those throws. He showed his toughness when (Khalil Mack) was bearing down on him. But I think the thing I'm most proud of is the job we did in the red zone. We came off a game that we were just OK and yet

Chicago Bears linebacker Kevin Pierre-Louis (57) tries to wrap up Chiefs running back Damien Williams (26) in the first half. NAM Y. HUH / AP PHOTO

Chiefs quarterback Patrick Mahomes (15) scores easily on a 12-yard touchdown run in the first quarter. JOE ROBBINS / AP PHOTO

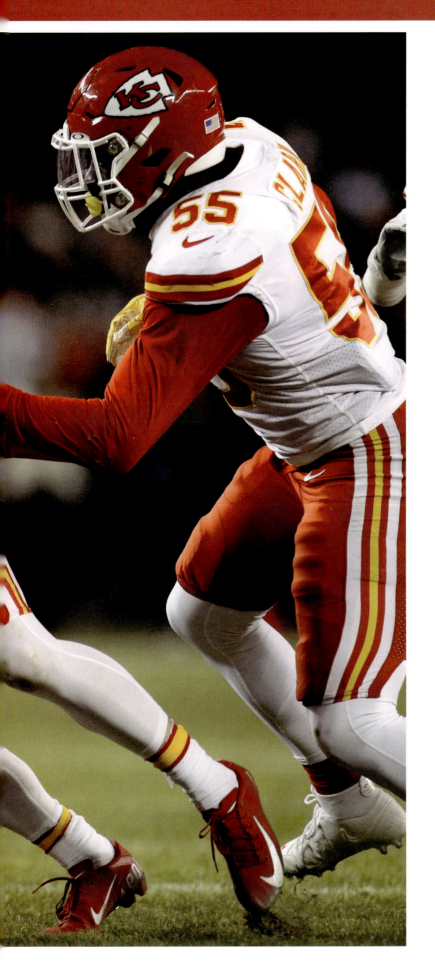

we were able to put it in down there."

Travis Kelce, already the first tight end with four straight 1,000-yard seasons, became the first to reach 1,200 yards in back-to-back years. He caught eight passes for 74 yards, giving him 1,205 this year. That included a 6-yard touchdown near the end of the first half.

Harrison Butker kicked a career-best 56-yard field goal that was the fourth-longest in franchise history. He also hit both the left and right uprights on a missed extra point.

"The team has a lot of momentum right now," Butker said. "We're feeling good and we've just been on a roll. The chemistry has been amazing and this is the perfect time to be kind of move upward and hitting on all strides."

The defense showed up in Chicago as well.

Kansas City has now held opponents under 18 points in five straight games. The Bears also became the third team in the past four to fail to top 10 points against the Chiefs, but the defense isn't satisfied with the postseason looming.

"Like I've said in previous weeks, we want to be able to not rely on our offense to finish a game," defensive tackle Derrick Nnadi said. "We want to be the type of defense that can finish a game" ∎

Chiefs defensive backs Daniel Sorensen (49) and Juan Thornhill (22) tackle Chicago Bears running back David Montgomery (32). JOE ROBBINS / AP PHOTO

KANSAS CITY 31, L.A. CHARGERS 21

DECEMBER 29, 2019 | KANSAS CITY, MISSOURI

A(nother) Defensive Gem

Chiefs earn No. 2 seed, first-round bye

Patrick Mahomes kept scrounging around the Kansas City sideline for a score update from New England, and all the Chiefs quarterback learned was that Tom Brady had thrown a touchdown pass and an interception against Miami.

That news blackout was by design.

Andy Reid didn't want anybody to know what was transpiring in Foxborough, where the Chiefs needed the Dolphins to spring a big upset Sunday for any hope of a first-round playoff bye. Instead, the Chiefs' coach wanted Mahomes and Co. to focus on beating the Chargers, a game they needed for the outcome in New England to have any consequence.

"There was no scoreboard at all that had any number of stats or anything like that," Mahomes said. "Then I saw that Brady had a touchdown and an interception and I was trying to add that together to figure out what the score was."

In the end, the two scores that mattered went Kansas City's way: The Chiefs beat the Chargers 31-21 behind big games from Mecole Hardman and Damien Williams, and the Dolphins rallied to stun the Patriots 27-24 in the closing seconds.

"I knew when the fans started to go crazy," Mahomes said with a smile. "It's basically a win, that's what it is. You win the first round of the playoffs and you get to play a home game. We're excited for that."

Mahomes had 174 yards passing and a touchdown in a relatively low-key performance, but his supporting cast picked up the slack. Hardman returned a kickoff 104 yards for a touchdown, Williams ran 84 yards for another score – and finished with 124 yards rushing and two TDs on just 12 carries – and the Chiefs (12-4) turned in another defensive gem.

Now, the Patriots have to play next week and the Chiefs can set their sights on the divisional round of the playoffs.

"The extra week off, it's great to have this time of year. You work hard for that," Reid said. "I'm proud of our guys for pushing through here today, because that's hard to do. You don't know the scores and you have to have the right mindset coming into this. The Dolphins were a 16-point underdog or whatever it was coming into this, but it's a great example of why you're playing. If you're on that field, you go 100 miles an hour and play your heart out."

The Chargers (5-11) made it stressful for

Chiefs free safety Tyrann Mathieu (32) goes up high for the interception. COOPER NEILL / AP PHOTO

Kansas City in the fourth quarter, though, driving for a touchdown that got them within 24-21 with 5:23 to go. But the Chiefs answered with an eight-play, 77-yard scoring drive that allowed them to wrap up their sixth straight win overall and 11th victory in 12 meetings with their longtime division rival.

They held Philip Rivers to 281 yards passing with two touchdowns and two interceptions in what could be the veteran quarterback's final game for the Chargers.

The Chiefs' offense has long been the headliner, but it has been their revamped defense under coordinator Steve Spagnuolo that has carried them on their current win streak. They had not allowed a touchdown the past two games, and Kansas City stretched that to 10 consecutive quarters when it forced a punt on the Chargers' initial possession.

The streak finally ended when Rivers found Keenan Allen in the end zone early in the second quarter.

The Chiefs regained the lead late in the half. Mahomes zipped a 30-yard strike to Hardman that set up a 24-yard TD pass to Demarcus Robinson, giving them a 10-7 advantage heading into the locker room.

"We don't plan on slowing down," Reid said. "We're going to keep our foot on the pedal and keep rolling." ∎

Chiefs defensive end Terrell Suggs (94) sacks Chargers quarterback Philip Rivers (17) during the second half. CHARLIE RIEDEL / AP PHOTO

Chiefs defensive end Chris Jones (95) and teammate Frank Clark (55) celebrate with the Kansas City faithful. CHARLIE RIEDEL / AP PHOTO

KANSAS CITY 51, HOUSTON 31

JANUARY 12, 2020 | KANSAS CITY, MISSOURI

A Comeback for the Ages

Chiefs rally from 24-0 hole to beat Texans

Patrick Mahomes stalked up and down the sideline like a field marshal rallying his troops, the brilliant young quarterback imploring the Kansas City Chiefs to stay together even as the Houston Texans were on the verge of taking them apart.

The Chiefs already faced a 24-0 hole, bigger than any deficit they had overcome in franchise history.

"The biggest thing I was preaching," Mahomes said later, "was, `Let's go do something special. Everybody is counting us out. Let's go out there and play by play put it out there.' And play by play, we did what we were supposed to do."

Beginning with the first of his five touchdown passes, Mahomes and the Chiefs slowly chipped away at Houston's seemingly insurmountable lead. They continued to pick up momentum, outscoring the Texans 28-0 during the second quarter alone, and eventually reeled off 41 consecutive points before cruising the rest of the way to a 51-31 victory Sunday that propelled Kansas City back to the AFC championship game for the second consecutive season.

In doing so, the Chiefs (13-4) became the first team in NFL history to win a playoff game by at least 20 points after trailing by at least 20. They matched the fourth-biggest comeback in playoff history while winning a postseason game in back-to-back seasons for the first time. Travis Kelce and Damien Williams scored three touchdowns apiece, joining the 49ers' Jerry Rice and Ricky Waters in Super Bowl 29 as the only teammates to score that many times in a postseason game.

Meanwhile, Mahomes led by example as much as by voice. He finished with 321 yards passing, becoming the first player in postseason history with at least 300 yards passing and five touchdowns while running for at least 50 more yards.

"You saw him going up and down the bench, he was talking to everybody, `Just settle down," Chiefs coach Andy Reid said. "As a head coach, you can't ask for more than that. When he's the leader of your team and he's going, `Hey, we're going to be fine. Let's not wait for the fourth quarter. Let's go!' And he did that."

Now, after losing to the Patriots in overtime in last year's conference title game, the Chiefs are back on the brink of their first Super Bowl appearance in 50 years.

Deshaun Watson, meanwhile, threw for 388 yards and two touchdowns while running for another, but not even his heroics could bail out the Texans (11-7) after their calamitous second quarter and dismal third. The result: The reborn Houston franchise is 0-4 in the divisional round and has never won a road playoff game.

"I definitely thought we were going to have to score more than 24," said Texans coach Bill O'Brien, who made a series of debatable

Chiefs running back Damien Williams (26) celebrates after scoring one of his two third quarter touchdowns. REED HOFFMANN / AP PHOTO

Chiefs quarterback Patrick Mahomes (15) scans the field. Mahomes threw 5 touchdowns on the day. AARON M. SPRECHER / AP PHOTO

ABOVE: Chiefs defensive back Daniel Sorensen (49) drags down Texans wide receiver Deandre Hopkins (10). REED HOFFMANN / AP PHOTO

RIGHT: Chiefs defensive back Bashaud Breeland (21) celebrates with the crowd late in the second half. REED HOFFMANN / AP PHOTO

calls during the collapse. "I think that they're, obviously, a very explosive team and it just didn't work out."

The Chiefs certainly gave Houston a chance to end their frustrating playoff streak in the first quarter.

On defense, Kansas City blew coverage on Kenny Stills on the opening possession, allowing him to walk into the end zone from 54 yards. On offense, they wasted timeouts, dropped a series of easy passes and managed just 46 yards. And on special teams, the Chiefs had a punt blocked for a score and fumbled a return that set up another touchdown.

Indeed, the Texans kept humming right along after finishing on a 22-3 run to beat Buffalo last week, while the mountain of miscues made by the Chiefs made them only the fourth home playoff team to trail 21-0 after the first quarter.

Things turned around on a series of plays – and a call by O'Brien in particular – that will be debated for a while.

After the Texans stretched the lead to 24-0 early in the second quarter, the Chiefs began to chip away at their deficit with a quick touchdown drive. And the comeback really gained momentum when O'Brien called for a fake punt at the Houston 31-yard line and the Chiefs stuffed it, giving them a short field and setting up another easy touchdown.

"We had that play ready for a variety of different teams and situations," said the Texans' Justin Reid, who took the snap and was stopped short of the first down. "Credit to them, they made the play."

As the Chiefs continued to take off, the Texans continued to stumble.

On the ensuing kickoff, Houston return man DeAndre Carter had the ball pop loose and into the arms of Darwin Thompson, whose recovery set up a second Mahomes-to-Kelce touchdown in a matter of seconds. And their third came after the Chiefs forced a punt – a successful one, for a change – and they drove 90 yards to take a stunning 28-24 halftime lead.

"I mean, it was an amazing thing. Everything was working," Mahomes said. "The play calls were open, everybody was getting open against man-coverage which we've been preaching all season long, and guys were making plays."

The comeback became a clobbering by the time the third quarter ended.

It also gave a festive crowd that turned out early in freezing weather and a slight drizzle a chance to celebrate early.

"We've got full confidence not only in the players but the game plan going into it. Just got to deal with what's going on in the game – what's real and what's not – and what was real was we were hurting ourselves early," Kelce said. "With that, you just rally the troops, lean on the leaders of this team and make plays. That's what we did." ∎

Chiefs running back Damien Williams (26) high steps into the end zone for another score. CHARLIE RIEDEL / AP PHOTO

KANSAS CITY 35, TENNESSEE 24
JANUARY 19, 2020 | KANSAS CITY, MISSOURI

Super Bowl Bound
Chiefs earn first trip to Super Bowl in 50 years

With his best imitation of a tightrope walker, Patrick Mahomes high-wired the Kansas City Chiefs into their first Super Bowl since 1970.

Oh sure, Mahomes did his usual superb job passing, but it was his 27-yard tap dance down the left sideline late in the first half that gave the Chiefs their first lead. From there, they outran the run-oriented Tennessee Titans and star back Derrick Henry for a 35-24 victory Sunday in the AFC championship.

At last, for the third time overall, the Chiefs (14-4) are Super Bowl bound.

"I mean, it's amazing. It really is," said Mahomes, who had 294 yards passing and three touchdowns. "To be here, to be a part of Chiefs Kingdom and to be able to do it here at Arrowhead, these people deserve it. And we're not done yet."

Adding to the joy of the achievement, coach Andy Reid and owner Clark Hunt accepted the Lamar Hunt Trophy – named after his father – emblematic of the AFC title. It was handed over to them by Chiefs Hall of Famer Bobby Bell, with Mahomes and safety Tyrann Mathieu jumping for joy on the makeshift stage.

Next up: chasing the Vince Lombardi Trophy.

"Very excited and very emotional to win the trophy that has my dad's name on it," Hunt said. "Yeah, 50 years were too long, but we're going to another Super Bowl.

"Chiefs Kingdom, we are going to the Super Bowl."

The Chiefs lost in 1967 in the first AFL-NFL Championship Game – nope, it wasn't called the Super Bowl yet – to the Lombardi led Packers 35-10. Three years later, one year after the New York Jets shocked Baltimore to lay claim to the AFL being equal to the long-established NFL, Kansas City was back. This time, it was known as the Super Bowl – indeed, Lamar Hunt is credited with coming up with the name – and his Chiefs hammered Minnesota 23-7 with the typical Wild West offensive flair and a staunch defense. Those are characteristics that helped carry KC this season.

Reid isn't as animated as Hall of Famer Hank Stram, who famously urged the Chiefs team to "keep matriculating the ball down the field, boys." Caught up in the moment Sunday, Reid said, "It's awesome," before asking the crowd to chant "How about those Chiefs?"

Moments later, standout tight end Travis Kelce proclaimed, "You gotta fight for your right to party."

Chiefs quarterback Patrick Mahomes holds up the Lamar Hunt Trophy. CHARLIE NEIBERGALL / AP PHOTO

ABOVE: Chiefs running back Damien Williams (26) dashes in the end zone for a fourth quarter score. PERRY KNOTTS / AP PHOTO

RIGHT: Chiefs receiver Tyreek Hill (10) catches a first quarter touchdown pass in front of Titans cornerback Logan Ryan to get Kansas City on the board. ED ZURGA / AP PHOTO

There will be plenty of partying on South Beach for Chiefs Kingdom heading into the championship matchup.

"Fired up to go to Miami, got to get on a diet so I can fit into my beach clothes," Reid said. "So much effort that went into this. It takes an army, it is not one guy at all. I appreciate the effort by everybody. Very proud of these guys."

As they had done in their past three "elimination" games, the sixth-seeded Titans (11-8) got started quickly. The difference at Arrowhead as opposed to Houston, New England and Baltimore was that the Chiefs had Mahomes, Tyreek Hill, Sammy Watkins and Damien Williams on offense, and a vastly upgraded defense from when they lost in last year's AFC title game. Henry was held to 7 yards rushing in the second half.

"They were doubling all these guys," Mahomes said of his spectacular TD run on which he barely stayed in bounds. "I just ran it and got some good blocking at the end and found a way to get in the end zone."

A week after they overcame a 24-0 deficit against Houston, the Chiefs had to rally again.

Down 10-0 and 17-7, Kansas City didn't flinch, building a 35-17 lead while controlling the clock with a strong ground game. Naturally, Mahomes complemented that with sharp passing, spreading the ball on short and deep throws. The dagger came with a 60-yard completion to Watkins for the Chiefs' 28th straight point midway in the final period.

Mahomes thrust both arms in the air as the crowd sang Whitney Houston's "I Wanna Dance With Somebody."

That somebody will be the San Francisco 49ers in two weeks.

After taking a 3-0 lead on Greg Joseph's first field goal – with Tennessee's penchant for scoring

Chiefs quarterback Patrick Mahomes (15) finishes off an incredible 27-yard touchdown run with :11 seconds left in the half while Titans defenders look on. PERRY KNOTTS / AP PHOTO

in the red zone, he hadn't been called upon in his previous four games with the team – the Titans got a huge break. Bashaud Breeland appeared to make a diving interception, but replay review showed the ball hitting the ground.

Helped by consecutive offside penalties and a a fourth-down pass to Adam Humphries for his first career playoff reception, the Titans converted on, what else, Henry's 4-yard run.

Then the Chiefs got rolling, scoring on three successive series. Hill took it in on a shovel pass, later beat top Titans cornerback Logan Ryan for a 20-yard reception, and Mahomes finished the half with his brilliant jaunt down the left sideline with half the Tennessee defense seemingly expecting him to step out of bounds.

That gave the Chiefs a 21-17 lead. It went to 28-17 on Williams' 3-yard run to cap a seven-minute drive. Then Watkins toasted Logan for the clinching long pass.

Henry was held to 69 yards on 19 carries after rushing for 588 yards in the past three games as an unstoppable force.

"I feel like our backs were against the wall the whole season," Henry said. "But we kept on fighting and kept on believing in each other. We just came up short." ∎

Chiefs head coach Andy Reid holds up the Lamar Hunt Trophy for the Kansas City crowd following the AFC Championship Game win.
G. NEWMAN LOWRANCE / AP PHOTO

Super Bowl 1970

A look back at the Chiefs' last Super Bowl appearance

The last time Kansas City claimed a title, founder and owner Lamar Hunt was leading the charge, and Kansas City was still part of the American Football League (AFL). Coach Hank Stram's Chiefs, a 13-point underdog, dominated the match-up with the Minnesota Vikings, 23-7, before 80,997 at Tulane Stadium on January 11, 1970.

The win was a total redemption for the Chiefs, who had been tabbed the goats of the inaugural Super Bowl, won by the Green Bay Packers, 35-10, in 1967. It was redemption for the AFL, which still had a few skeptics to convince about its parity with the NFL, even after the Jets' stunning upset over the Colts the year before. And it was redemption for quarterback Len Dawson, who called a tremendous game in picking apart the Vikings in completing 12 of 17 passes for 142 yards and a touchdown, and who wound up winning a Dodge Challenger sports car as Sport Magazine's outstanding player in the championship game. Members of the winning team were paid $15,000-per-man.

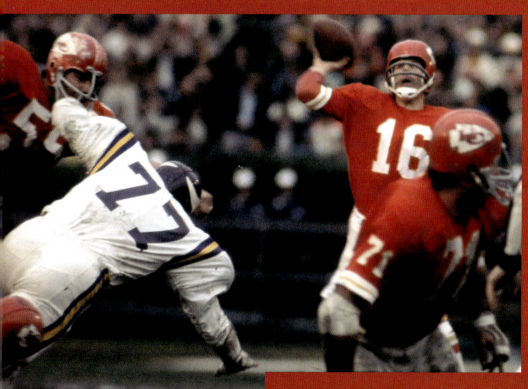

LEFT: Chiefs quarterback Len Dawson (16) gets set to throw a pass under pressure from the Vikings defense.

LOWER LEFT: Head coach Hank Stram poses with the Lombardi Trophy.

BELOW: Hall of Fame defensive tackles Curley Culp (61) and Buck Buchanan (86) tackle Vikings running back Dave Osborn (41).

LOWER: A ticket for Super Bowl IV.

OPPOSITE: Hall of Fame place kicker Jan Stenerud (3) kicks one of his three field goals on the day.

PHOTOS COURTESY AP IMAGES

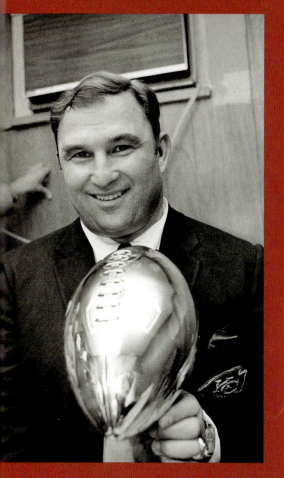

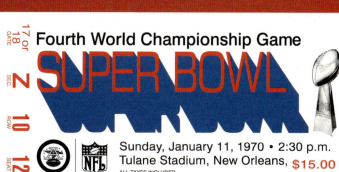

2019 ROSTER

OFFENSE

NO.	NAME	POS.	HT.	WT.	AGE	EXP	HOMETOWN
4	Chad Henne	QB	6'3"	222 lbs	34	12	Michigan
15	Patrick Mahomes	QB	6'3"	230 lbs	24	3	Texas Tech
8	Matt Moore	QB	6'3"	219 lbs	35	12	Oregon State
25	LeSean McCoy	RB	5'11"	210 lbs	31	11	Pittsburgh
34	Darwin Thompson	RB	5'8"	200 lbs	22	R	Utah State
26	Damien Williams	RB	5'11"	224 lbs	27	6	Oklahoma
42	Anthony Sherman	FB	5'10"	242 lbs	31	9	Connecticut
17	Mecole Hardman	WR	5'10"	187 lbs	21	R	Georgia
10	Tyreek Hill	WR	5'10"	185 lbs	25	4	West Alabama
13	Byron Pringle	WR	6'1"	203 lbs	26	2	Kansas State
11	Demarcus Robinson	WR	6'1"	203 lbs	25	4	Florida
14	Sammy Watkins	WR	6'1"	211 lbs	26	6	Clemson
81	Blake Bell	TE	6'6"	252 lbs	28	5	Oklahoma
87	Travis Kelce	TE	6'5"	260 lbs	30	7	Cincinnati
82	Deon Yelder	TE	6'4"	255 lbs	24	2	Western Kentucky
62	Austin Reiter	C	6'3"	300 lbs	28	4	South Florida
73	Nick Allegretti	G	6'4"	320 lbs	23	R	Illinois
76	Laurent Duvernay-Tardif	G	6'5"	321 lbs	28	6	McGill
60	Ryan Hunter	G	6'3"	316 lbs	24	1	Bowling Green
61	Stefen Wisniewski	G	6'3"	305 lbs	30	9	Penn State
77	Andrew Wylie	G	6'6"	309 lbs	25	2	Eastern Michigan
68	Jackson Barton	OT	6'7"	302 lbs	24	R	Utah
75	Cam Erving	OT	6'5"	313 lbs	27	5	Florida State
72	Eric Fisher	OT	6'7"	315 lbs	29	7	Central Michigan
71	Mitchell Schwartz	OT	6'5"	320 lbs	30	8	California

DEFENSE

NO.	NAME	POS.	HT.	WT.	AGE	EXP	HOMETOWN
55	Frank Clark	DE	6'3"	260 lbs	26	5	Michigan
92	Tanoh Kpassagnon	DE	6'7"	289 lbs	25	3	Villanova
94	Terrell Suggs	DE	6'3"	265 lbs	37	17	Arizona State
95	Chris Jones	DT	6'6"	310 lbs	25	4	Mississippi State
91	Derrick Nnadi	DT	6'1"	312 lbs	23	2	Florida State
64	Mike Pennel	DT	6'4"	332 lbs	28	6	Colorado State-Pueblo
99	Khalen Saunders	DT	6'0"	324 lbs	23	R	Western Illinois
98	Xavier Williams	DT	6'2"	309 lbs	28	5	Northern Iowa
52	Demone Harris	LB	6'4"	272 lbs	24	1	Buffalo
53	Anthony Hitchens	LB	6'0"	235 lbs	27	6	Iowa
50	Darron Lee	LB	6'1"	232 lbs	25	4	Ohio State
56	Ben Niemann	LB	6'2"	235 lbs	24	2	Iowa
44	Dorian O'Daniel	LB	6'1"	220 lbs	25	2	Clemson
59	Reggie Ragland	LB	6'2"	252 lbs	26	4	Alabama
54	Damien Wilson	LB	6'0"	245 lbs	26	5	Minnesota
21	Bashaud Breeland	CB	5'11"	195 lbs	27	6	Clemson
30	Alex Brown	CB	5'9"	183 lbs	23	R	South Carolina State
20	Morris Claiborne	CB	5'11"	192 lbs	29	8	LSU
27	Rashad Fenton	CB	5'11"	188 lbs	22	R	South Carolina
29	Kendall Fuller	CB	5'11"	198 lbs	24	4	Virginia Tech
35	Charvarius Ward	CB	6'1"	198 lbs	23	2	Middle Tennessee
24	Jordan Lucas	S	6'1"	190 lbs	26	4	Penn State
32	Tyrann Mathieu	S	5'9"	190 lbs	27	7	LSU
49	Daniel Sorensen	S	6'2"	208 lbs	29	6	BYU
23	Armani Watts	S	5'11"	205 lbs	23	2	Texas A&M

SPECIAL TEAMS

NO.	NAME	POS	HT	WT	AGE	EXP	COLLEGE
7	Harrison Butker	PK	6'4"	205 lbs	24	3	Georgia Tech
2	Dustin Colquitt	P	6'3"	210 lbs	37	15	Tennessee
41	James Winchester	LS	6'3"	240 lbs	30	5	Oklahoma